In the
NICK
of TIME

ALSO BY

DR. SHERRY L. MEINBERG

Alzheimer's ABC

*A Cluster of Cancers: A Simple
Coping Guide for Patients*

Seizing the Teachable Moment

The Cockroach Invasion

Breadcrumbs for Beginners: Following the Writing Trail

Diabetes ABC

Imperfect Weddings are Best

*Recess is Over! No Nonsense Strategies and Tips
For Student Teachers and New Teachers*

*It's All Thought! The Science, Psychology, and
Spirituality of Happiness* (Teachers Guide)

Autism ABC

The Bogeyman: Stalking and its Aftermath

(TV Premier Episode, Investigation
Discovery, 12/12/12)

*Toxic Attention: Keeping Safe from
Stalkers, Abusers, and Intruders*

Be the Boss of Your Brain! Take Control of Your Life

Chicken Soup for the Kid's Soul (Story)

*Into the Hornet's Nest: An Incredible Look
at Life in an Inner City School*

In the NICK *of* TIME

Coincidences, Synchronicities,
Dreams, Signs and Symbols

Dr. Sherry L. Meinberg

authorHOUSE®

AuthorHouse™
1663 Liberty Drive
Bloomington, IN 47403
www.authorhouse.com
Phone: 1 (800) 839-8640

Published by AuthorHouse   07/07/2016

ISBN: 978-1-5246-1647-2 (sc)
ISBN: 978-1-5246-1646-5 (e)

Library of Congress Control Number: 2016908911

Print information available on the last page.

Any people depicted in stock imagery provided by Thinkstock are models,
and such images are being used for illustrative purposes only.
Certain stock imagery © Thinkstock.

This book is printed on acid-free paper.

DEDICATION

This book is dedicated to you, the reader. I happily invite you to walk with me, as I share my eighty personal stories, regarding coincidences, synchronicities, dreams, signs, and symbols. Trust me: At the outset of this project, this was not meant to be a me-me-me book. But no one—family, friends, neighbors, or strangers—said that they had had any synchronicity experiences, and all said that they had common examples of coincidence. So it turns out that each and every example is mine (if you count the two of my husband and sons). As such, I'm encouraging you to pause and consider, pause and consider . . . , and *remember* your own personal encounters. I hope you connect with my once-over-lightly show and tell.

CONTENTS

CONTENTS

IN THE NICK OF TIME

Just in time;
at the exact right time;
at the last possible moment;
in the final instant;
under the wire;
at a vital moment;
split second timing;
just before the deadline;
in a heartbeat;
in the blink of an eye;
in a flash;
suddenly;
just before the last minute
when something can be changed
or else something bad will happen.

—Synonyms

FOREWORD

Sooner or later, out-of-the-blue, unusual, unexpected, mind-blowing situations happen, that can startle you out of your everyday life. The split-second timing is amazingly unbelievable. You acknowledge that something significant has occurred, although you might not know exactly what it is. Such events are powerful, and can change the course of your life, and even transform it. Such experiences can be your own little miracles. Note that all of the examples throughout the following pages, have to do with *timing*, in one way or another.

COINCIDENCE

*Coincidence is the word we use
when we can't see
the levers and pulleys.*

—Emma Bull

COINCIDENCE

*When you live your life
with an appreciation of coincidences . . .
you connect with the underlying field of
infinite possibilities.*
—Deepak Chopra

A coincidence is when two unplanned events happen simultaneously, meaning nothing particular in itself. They do not seem to have much effect on you, either emotionally or intellectually, as the content is of minor import. There is no preparation, technique, nor conscious effort involved. Coincidences just happen out-of-the-blue.

Small coincidences are commonplace. They happen so often that most people won't even waste a second thinking about them. They may not even be recognized, or thought of, as unusual. They tend to be dismissed, overlooked, shrugged off, or ignored, since they are not a Thunderbolt Experience. Kind of like dreams. Susan M. Watkins, in her book, *What a Coincidence!*, suggests that coincidences are the wide-awake extensions of the dream state, and, as such, readers should be attentive to both. She says, "Maybe coincidences are always there, muttering in the background, forming the Internet of our days, a media hullabaloo of their own."

Everyone has had the experience of coincidence, now and then. Common garden variety coincidences include thinking of a person, and the phone rings, and that particular person is calling you; or bumping into a friend that was on your mind; or thinking of a long-lost individual, and receiving a letter or email from him or her; or two people saying the same thing aloud, at the same time. My brother and I are often trading emails on the same day, at the same time. Such events are acausal events, meaning not involving causation, or not arising from a cause. One event does not cause the other. No rhyme or reason seems to be involved in such oddball connections and encounters, as there is no direct cause-and-effect relationship.

Coincidental experiences are often called a fluke or happenstance, or quirks of fate, occurring by chance, or by luck. Many people enjoy the instant connection, laugh at such a situation, and then promptly forget about it. Coincidences are often described as tiny blessings, precious gifts, little bulletins from God, a secret handshake from the universe, and God shots. Some are called kissing cousins to miracles, whereas others just call them hellos from heaven.

VISIT

My aunt and uncle came to visit us in California from Texas. We took them to see Knott's Berry Farm, a 160-acre amusement park, with over 165 rides, dozens of shows, and various attractions. It is a hugely popular entertainment site, with the average number of daily visitors at **10,000**. While in the park's crowded Old West Gold Town section, in that whole mass of strangers, my uncle accidently bumped into a neighbor (who owned the ranch next to his). Neither knew that the other was also visiting California. "What a coincidence!" everyone laughed. "It's a small world, after all."

David Spangler shows, in his *Everyday Miracles* book, that coincidences affirm that we are all connected in subtle and wonderful ways. It is said that such chance encounters do not exist. When people cross your path, there is always a reason, and there is always a message for you (and/or them). Afterwards, stop and give your unexpected meeting some thought. Look beyond whatever drama was involved. Know that every event has significance. Look for the silver lining. (I thought that "the silver lining" was just a poetic term, until I actually saw a beautiful silver lining around a cloud one day. It was absolutely gorgeous, and the image stayed in my mind for months. I hope to see one again.)

Such seemingly unrelated coincidences may simply point out the underlying message of *connection*; that all the phenomena about you is interconnected, interrelated, and interactive; recognize the inseparability of all things; that we are all connected to the same switchboard. At its core, everything is united. Life is a unified field, a oneness, according to Albert Einstein, Ph.D. And the theoretical physicist, David Bohm, Ph.D., agrees, suggesting a primal state of oneness ("the implicate order"), saying that "Deep down, the consciousness of mankind is one." "We connect with everyone and everything in the universe," adds Deepak Chopra. "We are all part of the cosmic quantum soup." Surely you've heard the theory that there are only six degrees of separation between all humans . . .

And, as John Muir observed: "When we try to pick out anything by itself, we find it is hitched to everything else in the universe." Everything is a part of everything else. Gay Hendrick, in his book *Conscious Living*, quotes the Zen author, D.T. Suzuki, when he called it, "the lightning-and-thunder discovery that the universe and oneself are not remote and apart, but an intimate, palpitating whole."

Or, a coincidence may simply show that you are on the same wavelength with another person. Or, a coincidence may "reaffirm that your existence is not random," giving you reassurance and confidence that you are not alone, and you are on the right track, as SQuire Rushnell tells us, in his little book, *When God Winks*.

On the other hand, if a stand-alone coincidence seems connected somehow to another—or if a series of events occurs, like a chain, or a beaded necklace, or a connected pipeline—and the cumulative impact of a *cluster* of coincidences is apparent, you would do well to consider the message. Chopra emphasizes that "Coincidences are like road flares, calling attention to something important in our lives . . ." Know that all such coincidences are signs. Chopra adds, "And the more unlikely the coincidence, the more potent the clue."

REPETITION

> Shortly before I received my cancer diagnosis, out-of-the-blue, in one week, I read two books, and saw three TV movies, in which cancer was the subject matter. (The word wasn't mentioned on the books' cover flaps, or in the TV preview ads. I *never* would have read or watched them, had I known). *How weird is that?* I thought to myself. *What a coincidence!* And didn't give it another thought. I didn't even have an inkling . . .

Such moments in life are not to be left "unnoticed or unexamined," Neale Donald Walsch maintains, in his book, *Moments of Grace*. But what did I know?

A singular coincidence may appear " . . . to have little or no comprehensible significance. However, if it begins to make sense when seen in the context of similar experiences, it can then be regarded as but one piece in a larger mosaic," suggests Frank Joseph, in *Synchronicity and You: Understanding the Role of Meaningful Coincidence in Your Life*. He kept a diary, over a four-year period, in which he recorded his coincidence experiences. It turned out that he received about 100 a year, on average eight times a month. Viewed separately, their significance was not always apparent. But seen in the broader context, of those that came before or after the event, they showed tremendous relevance.

Bernard D. Beitman, M.D.—a visiting psychiatry professor at the University of Virginia—tells us in his book, *Connecting with Coincidence*, that, "You don't have to know how electricity works to flip the light switch and turn on the light in the room. Likewise, you don't have to understand how a coincidence works to be able to use it to improve your life."

Experts tell us that being on the lookout for coincidences can attract them to you; that whatever is expected tends to be realized. Chopra says, "The more attention you put on coincidences, the more you attract other coincidences." Halberstam and Leventhal agree, in *Small Miracles II*, saying "When you believe in coincidences, they pour into your life at an exhilarating, almost dizzying rate." Dr. Kirby Surprise also says, "An attitude of expectancy greatly increases the number of events you experience." And Dr. Bernie Siegel writes, in his preface to *Small Miracles*, "Behave as if you have coincidences in your life, expect them, and when you are ready to receive them, they'll come," as the following examples suggest:

CONNECTIONS

At the exact moment, when I was typing the phrase, "thinking of a person and the phone rings, and that particular person is calling you," my phone rang. The caller was an old friend from Minnesota, that I hadn't heard from in a very, very long time, and she had been strongly on my mind.

A sister-in-law wrote me an extra long email, starting out with: "This is the truth. I was just thinking of you when Terry (my brother) called to say you needed my address. Wow!"

When my phone rang early one morning, I knew it was my dentist. It was. He called to tell me that he was having a bout with vertigo, and had been in bed for two days. So he (instead of his office manager) canceled my appointment.

When I was typing the Funeral story for a later chapter, a call came in from a relative, with the long-expected news that a family member had died from a lengthy bout with cancer. Directly thereafter, another phone call from my son came in, to tell me that his close friend and landlord had just died from a totally unexpected heart attack.

I had decided to take a break from writing this chapter for a few minutes, and picked up David Baldacci's latest mystery, *The Last Mile* (2016). I no more than resumed my recreational reading, when on the bottom of page 221, several words got my attention: *coincidence* and *in the nick of time*. I took that as a validation. Later, as I was reading *The Search for 11:11* (2004), by George Mathieu Barnard, I came across *in the nick of time* (p. 15), *coincidences* (p. 88), and *in a blink-of-an-eye* (p. 122). Even more validations. And with the new Craig Johnson's book (2016), *The Highwayman* (a Longmire story), were the words (on page 162), " . . . a miracle of synchronicity." I take support and confirmation wherever I can find them.

"Coincidence is instructive," says Dr. David Richo, in his book, *Unexpected Miracles*. "The psyche will direct us to the exact information that we need when we need it." I can testify to that:

CONDUIT

When writing the First Day story in the Synchronicity chapter, I typed the word *conduit* in the sentence, "I was just a conduit of information, but the message had great meaning for both involved." And I wondered if I should use another word instead, as I hadn't seen or heard the word in ages. A short time later, I was reading *Manifesting Michelangelo*, by Joseph Pierce Farrell, " . . . Luciano Pavarotti also gave credit to Spirit for his brilliant operatic performances. Pavarotti always said that he was just a *conduit for the* Divine." (pp. 63-64). Later, I was reading *Solomon Speaks* on *Reconnecting Your Life*, by Dr. Eric Pearl and Frederick Ponzlov, and came upon the word *conduit* on two different pages (pp. 51 & 177). The latter page said, "Your role is purely to be a *conduit*. It's an important role. Make no mistake about it. Make no mistake about it." Even Abigail Van Buren, in her Dear Abby column, said "The interpreter is not considered to be part of the conversation, just a 'conduit.'" Wow! I took all of the above as validation that I could safely use the word without any misunderstanding.

So, I was in the midst of writing this section about coincidences, and each day another coincidence happened. Coincidences often appear in a repetition of events.

SIX REPETITIONS

One day, I was leaving for a meeting with a new group I had just joined: CalRTA (the California Retired Teachers Association). I was sure that I wouldn't know anybody there, since it had been twenty-one years since I had retired from the district. As I was going out the door, my husband said, "Tell them you're *famous*!" And I replied, "Oh, sure, I'm going to throw up my arms and yell, "I'm *famous*!" Famous, indeed, I laughingly grumbled, as I left.

(1) I wasn't prepared for the number of people at the meeting site. There were

24 tables of eight (192). I no more than walked into the room, when a woman grabbed hold of me, then threw up her arms, and said, "Sherry, you're *famous*! I tell everyone that I know you!" (I recognized her name—printed on her name tag—but couldn't place which school I knew her from.)

(2) Then the meeting started, so I had to find an empty seat. I sat at the back table, with two empty chairs next to me. And in walked a couple that I knew from Monroe Elementary School, some 30-plus years prior. Dale recognized me right away. (I had to put on my glasses to recognize them.) Then, his wife, Jan, excitedly said, "You're *famous*! We read about you all the time!" All I could do was laugh. No one had ever called me famous to my face before. And now three people in one day! *How fun is that?*

(3) I emailed my brother to tell him the story. He responded, "Wow. *Famous* sister! Ha!" as he proceeded to remind me not to believe my own BS.

(4) Several days later, my nephew brought his wife, and two children

down to visit us in California. We briefly talked about my 14 published books. Later, as they were driving back to Oregon, I emailed him to say that my recent *Cluster of Cancers* book had just won two more awards. And seven-year-old Liam said, "Dad, is your aunt *famous*?"

(5) A couple of days later, my husband and I flew to Las Vegas to celebrate his birthday. As we were walking through the casino, we were chatting with a couple of strangers, when the woman said that they had just found out that their two-year-old grandson had been diagnosed with autism. We talked about my *Autism ABC* book, when she suddenly yelled, "You're *famous*! You're famous! You are the second famous person I've met on this trip! The first was a woman Olympic weight-lifter we met on the plane, and the second is *you*!" And she proceeded to call her daughter, and told her to order the book on Amazon. And her daughter was quite excited to do so. Late the next evening, I was going up to my room, and as I was getting on the packed elevator, there was the same woman again. "She's FAMOUS!" she yelled, pointing at me,

while proceeding to tell everyone that I was a famous writer.

(6) To take it one step further: I had ordered Sophy Burnham's book, *The Art of Intuition*, from Amazon, and it had arrived in the mail, just after we returned from Las Vegas. Eager to read it, I dove right in. And on the very first page of the first chapter, were the words, "You're going to be famous." Wow!

Jeez, Louise! I simply couldn't believe it. Within a two-week period, I had heard the word *famous* more than anytime, altogether, in my whole entire life, and it was connected to me. *How weird is that?*

Often times, whatever you are focused on, or dealing with, brings about surprising coincidental experiences. For instance:

ANOTHER SIX REPETITIONS

(1) I was putting together the chapter on Colors, and my newspaper horoscope for the day said: Let your imagination color the scene.

(2) And I came across a comic strip, *The Argyle Sweater*, by Scott Hilburn, showing two chameleons having a discussion, called:

CHAMELEON GOSSIP

Chameleon #1: When I asked to borrow a few bucks, boy did Audrey show her true colors.

Chameleon #2: Oooh . . .What were they?

Chameleon #1: It was kind of an olive-pine.

(3) Five different strangers (four clients at a nail salon, and one waitress), as well as my own brother—and apropos of nothing—all individually said, "I really like the color of your hair." (I made it a point to tell my hairdresser!)

(4) While rereading Brendon Burchard's *The Charge*, I came across: " . . . desire more color, variety, creativity, freedom, and connection."

(5) On the anniversary of my 8th year of being cancer free, I received a copy of the *Cancer Fighters Thrive* magazine. Talk about timing!

(6) And on the magazine's last pages (49-50) was a coloring activity, called

"Coloring Your World," which included the very same quote that I had used, by Georgia O'Keeffe about color, in my later chapter on Color.

Oddly, a repetition may occur over several years time, such as the following:

LOVE AND MARRIAGE

One day in 2015, my husband and I were quietly eating at Baja Sonora, a popular Mexican restaurant, in Long Beach, California. At one point, Wayne leaned across the table, and whispered, "I love you." And a woman sitting at the next table went nuts! She stood up and pointed at us. *"Did you hear that?"* she announced, in a voice to declare the end of the world. *"Did you hear that?* For no reason at all, he just said, 'I love you,' while they were eating!" And she continued on in this manner. Of course, everyone stopped eating, and stared at us. Some quietly asked if we were dating, while others asked if we were newly weds. Then Wayne felt duty bound to explain to our audience that we were married, and had been together for 48 years. Shock and awe. Then, when they couldn't believe it, he followed with, "And this is the *third* marriage for both of us!" No one could believe that either. So much for peace and quiet.

A year later, in 2016, we were eating at The Claim Jumper in the Golden Nugget Casino, in Las Vegas. Five people stood around the next booth in which four others were seated. They were all discussing the upcoming nuptials of the blushing bride-to-be. As the five started to leave, Wayne asked about the wedding. He wanted to promote my book, *Imperfect Weddings Are Best*, but they all interrupted, asking if we were going to get married, or if we were newlyweds. We both responded, in unison, that we were married, and had been together for 49 years. Shock and awe. No one could believe it. Then they gathered their thoughts enough to say, "Congratulations!" and "What an accomplishment!" and so forth. It was déjà vu all over again!

"Stay alert," James Redfield says, in *The Celestine Prophecy*, as he urges readers to become conscious of the coincidences in our lives, and take them seriously. "Coincidences will occur regularly, but you have to notice them." As Walsch advises, "Don't *miss* life while you are *living* life." He further suggests that you increase your openness to new ideas, new possibilities, and new ways of understanding. Beitman notes that "Coincidences alert us to the mysterious hiding in plain sight." And Redfield agrees, "These coincidences make us feel there is something more, something spiritual, operating underneath everything we do, or operating behind the scenes." He adds: "The findings of physics, psychology, mysticism, and religion are all coming together into a new synthesis, based on a perception of the coincidences."

> *Coincidence is God's Way*
> *of remaining anonymous.*
> —Albert Einstein

SYNCHRONICITY

Synchronicity is more than a happy accident. It is an effect of the connectivity of the universe. It is proof that everything is a part of a unified, connected whole. It is an affirmation of life.

—David Wilcock

SYNCHRONICITY

*Synchronicity is an ever present reality
for those who have eyes to see.*
—Carl Jung

Synchronicities are unusual, unplanned, and unexpected experiences. They come in a way, and at a time, that you could not have anticipated or imagined. "Synchronicities cannot be consciously created. They take you by surprise," says Carol Lynn Pearson. Unlike coincidences, synchronicities are *meaningful* events that are deeply personal to you; a chance occurrence that is significant. Synchronicities are special moments; such events can change and transform you. "What seemed random and meaningless actually turns out to have been quite important," says Robert H. Hopcke, MFT. Synchronicity events have an *emotional* impact.

As Mary Soliel points out in her book, *I Can See Clearly Now,* "Some of us shine academically, some shine with street smarts, some shine creatively—every mind shines in its own way." As such, since you have a different background, different talents, and different questions, observations, and experiences, you are as unique as your fingerprints. So your synchronicities are personal messages that are meaningful only to you as an individual. Richo maintains that " . . . meaningfulness is always the ultimate criterion of synchronicity," saying that "synchronicity events are connected by meaning rather than by cause and effect." As such, stay alert to guidance in a different form.

"Synchronicities awaken you to the miraculous," say Trish and Rob MacGregor, in *Synchronicity and the Other Side*, their second book on the subject. Synchronicities are often called gifts from the Universe, godwinks, small miracles, post-it notes from above, moments of grace, nudges from heaven, and Divine Intervention. Soliel, continues, saying that "Synchronicity is God winking at us. When we notice it, we are winking right back."

It is said that synchronicity is the essence of timing. It involves a crucial time element. Such events are perfectly timed, to give guidance and direction. "They underline, italicize, and emphasize strong messages that we might otherwise ignore," offers Albert Clayton Gaulden, in his book, *Signs and Wonders*.

Synchronicities involve incredible odds that stagger the imagination. Know that if your experience defies probability, it is synchronistic, showing that more is involved than can be accounted for by chance. The odds seem "incalculable, representing a thing beyond probability," explains Joseph. Don't analyze the workings of it. Trying even to consider the odds will just make your head hurt, and waste your time. There are no explanations for it. As Linn says, "Sometimes it's best to accept the unexplainable without searching for a rational explanation." I wholeheartedly agree. ("There are a lot more things in heaven and earth, Horatio, than are dreamt of in your philosophy."—Shakespeare.)

"One of the hallmarks of a synchronistic event is that it is always unique and unrepeatable, a once-in-a-lifetime experience." And, further, "It seems that the cosmos has orchestrated this or that event just for your own private viewing," says Dr. Kirby Surprise, in his book, *Synchronicity*.

Sometimes it may be difficult to differentiate between the important, the trivial, and the insignificant. So take a tip from Alex Marcoux. She assures us, in her book, *Lifesigns*, that " . . . the more improbable the event, the more significant the meaning." As such, each example below demonstrates the three indicators for synchronicity: deep personal meaning, and crucial timing, which clearly defies probability.

WHAT ARE THE ODDS?

Having been an educator for over 50 years, it has been my observation that administrators sometimes make decisions, not realizing the havoc that will ensue down the line. One such decision happened in the old

Norwalk-La Mirada School District, in which my mother was a teacher. A boss had made the decision that all the newly built schools should use the old furniture, and the older schools would use the new furniture. It sounded fair to him (whereas, obviously, neither the aesthetics of the situation, nor fit, nor match, were of concern to him.) Unfortunately, no one told the teachers of this turn of events.

At the time, I was attending CSULB for a teaching degree, and was working as a recreation leader during summer vacation, at a newly built school in the city of La Mirada. One day, I just happened to walk off the playground, on my way to the office, when I passed two burly workmen, who were moving a huge, extremely heavy, chest-of-drawers. As the guys struggled by, one started to lose his grip, and as the chest tipped, the top drawer slid open, spilling charts, posters, artwork, and numerous papers at my feet. The chest was quickly set down, as I ran over to help pick up the mess. As I retrieved each item, I became confused and concerned, recognizing that the items all belonged to my mother, who taught second grade, at another school, in the city of Norwalk. I even came across a couple of charts and art project examples that *I* had made!

I asked the movers what they were doing with the chest, and they explained the recent directive from on high. I ran to the office, and called my mother in Long Beach, to explain the situation. She, in turn, called all of her colleagues (in various cities), who then descended upon the new school en masse, to retrieve all of their teaching possessions. What a disaster!

If I hadn't been walking past the workmen on that particular day, at that particular school, at that particular moment, none of the teachers would have had any idea in September, where all their personal school charts, posters, lesson plans, books, maps, and realia had gone. Timing is everything!

After the whole experience was over, I pondered the precise, split second timing that involved three cities. The mathematical odds of this happening are astounding. This event seemed to defy explanation. A minute either way, or taking another sidewalk (as I *always* did previously), would have completely changed the outcome. The timing involved is staggering, and simply takes my breath away. Richo agrees, saying: "The fact that just the right people appeared at just the right time in just the right place is a dazzling synchronicity." Oddly, a similar situation took place a number years later:

ARTWORK

During the early seventies, I was obsessively into art. I spent time in museums, art galleries, art shows, and art festivals. My walls were covered with original paintings and reproductions. (I even later became a docent at the CSULB Art Museum.) I mostly lamented the fact that I couldn't afford the pieces that really spoke to me.

One year, I was looking for a second job. So I showed up for a modeling interview, but realized that the opportunity would conflict with my teaching schedule. The modeling agency interviews were being conducted in a large back room staging area, which could only be reached through a large front room. It had been rented for a short period of time, as an art showroom, for a rising, talented artist: Kirwan.

I was stunned, upon realizing that I had stumbled into something totally unexpected: a private art party. Oh, boy, this was my kind of place! The room was packed with people roaming around, drinking champagne, while intensely discussing the various works on display. I happily made the tour, and was totally fascinated with the wildly intricate paintings on display. Wow!

I could hardly contain my enthusiasm when I came upon a huge lithograph, titled *Mr. Dark*, which is based on the character in Ray Bradbury's book, *Something Wicked This Way Comes*. I immediately bought a copy (#38/100, 1973) from Kirwan, himself. I later had it framed, which was extremely difficult to do, because of its size (42" x 84"), as well as the thin paper involved. This particular pencil drawing took Kirwan three months to complete, as the figure of the man has 317 separate images tattooed on his body, as seen through his suit. (Bradbury's head is shown on the lower left leg, and Kirwan's head is shown on the lower right leg. Very unusual.) It has been an outstanding conversation piece, all these years hence.

Six or so months thereafter, I drove from Long Beach into Los Angeles, where a yearly art fair was taking place. Several streets were closed to traffic, in that area, to accommodate the crowds. Artists set up shop on sidewalks, on the grassy areas, and in the middle of the streets, showing their various wares and talents. It was quite a colorful, happy, and energetic group.

As I wandered about, I came to a sudden halt in front of a little framed picture, showing two feet. It looked like one of Kirwan's, that I had seen. I then asked about the picture, since no artist's name was signed. None of the other pictures in the pile were autographed either. I quizzed the elderly couple as to the name of the artist involved, and was not satisfied with their answers. I left with a bad taste in my mouth.

On the long drive home, I agitated about it, and decided to call Kirwan, in Culver City, although I figured it was a lost cause. This meant that I was going to have to take some time to find his phone number (if I even had it). In addition, if we did connect, I might have to suffer the indignity of feeling foolish for bothering him, if nothing was wrong. But, I overrode my misgivings, and persevered.

Luckily, I found the number, and luckily Kirwan answered. I nervously introduced myself, starting out with, "You won't remember me, but I was at your show in Long Beach, over a half-year ago, and I bought your *"Mr. Dark . . ."*

"Oh, I remember *you*!" he interrupted, and proceeded to describe the outfit that I had been wearing that day, which shocked me silly. Then I haltingly spilled out my story. He freaked at that, and, in a mad rush, told me that, several months prior, his art studio had been broken into, and sixty thousand dollars worth of his paintings had been stolen. He said he was going to call the police right that minute, and he'd call me back, at a later date, when he had news.

Several days later, Kirwan did call me back, to tell me that the elderly couple had been so nervous about my questions, that they quickly packed up their belongings and left the fair, soon after I departed. But the organizers of the event had their names, and

information, so the police were able
to track them down. As such, Kirwan
was able to retrieve most of his stolen
artwork. He was so grateful, he promised
me a painting as a reward.

Again, I had arrived in the right place, at the
right time, with the right solution. And again, three
cities were involved. *How weird is that?* Sometimes
it's hard to grapple with the possible odds of a
situation.

Regarding Kirwan's artwork: You may have seen
some of his images, as he has since become known
nationally, and internationally, starting in the mid-
1970's. His prolific work takes the form of paintings,
posters, prints, puzzles, book covers, games,
calendars, architectural design, and sculpture. His
unusual, controversial, and sometimes disturbing
pieces are surrealistic, humanistic, and political. He
is also available for commissions. Check out his
website: Kirwan Studios.

EMERGENCY

My parents had never visited my
apartment. So it was quite surprising
when my mother dropped by one hot
July day. I was proud to present my
brand new two-week old baby to her,
as I placed Jay in her arms. (Of course,
she and my father had seen Jay through

the hospital glass windows, but didn't get to hold him.) At once, she became concerned about her grandson, asking me about his soft-spot. (*Soft-spot? What the heck was that?* I knew next to nothing about babies, having never been around them for any length of time, so this was a whole new experience for me. I was clueless.) Mother took immediate charge of the situation, and called the local hospital, explaining that I would bring Jay immediately, while the doctors cleared their schedules, to make way for an emergency operation.

Mother informed me that she would follow me to the hospital, and leave from there to drive home, after the situation was taken care of. I then explained that my car had been stolen a couple of days prior, and that I had no way to get to the hospital, so she took us there. (My husband was at work on a late shift, and he had had to rely on friends to drive him to and from the site, since the loss of our only vehicle, so he was unavailable, also.)

When Mother and I arrived at the hospital, everything had been cleared for the operation. Other operations had been canceled, and specific personnel were ready and waiting. Then I was asked for my insurance, and everything skidded to a stop. I told them that my insurance was through my school district. I was then informed that said insurance didn't cover women on pregnancy leave. *Say what?!* (This was in the 60's, and things were different then.) And furthermore, since it was my summer vacation, I wouldn't go back to work until September, so they were unsure of any future income. (They said that I could easily quit my job and move to another state. *Say what?!)* My husband wasn't insured through his work either, so the hospital refused Jay's admittance, because, to all intents and purposes, we were dead broke.

I was in some kind of a shocked state, in total disbelief that a hospital would refuse to admit a child in an obvious emergency situation, as Mother called around to other local hospitals, to no avail. They all required insurance. Jay was finally admitted to a hospital in another city, that dealt with the indigent and charity cases. And, since we had no car, we couldn't visit him every day. Luckily, Jay was only a few weeks old, and, wouldn't feel that his parents had deserted him.

I was a basket case during this period, and worried about the timing involved in this event. If my mother hadn't visited on that specific day, what might have happened? I shudder to think about it. Gaulden says that " . . . it is not important to know the reasons why everything happens in the amazing world of synchronicity." And Walsch tells us that his definition of a miracle is, " . . . just exactly the right thing, in just exactly the right way, at just exactly the right time." Sounds true for me. I have great empathy for what the unemployed go through, in similar situations.

PEERING THROUGH A WINDOW

Throughout my youth, I wanted to be a teacher when I grew up. So every morning, before I went to school in the 2nd grade, I dressed my dolls, and placed them on my bed (which I pretended was their school), and surrounded them with little books that I had made for them. Then (as their mother), I pretended to go to work and teach (like my mother and my father).

From junior high on, I would critique my teachers, during their daily lessons.

I knew what they could have said to interest the sport-minded, or the popular kids, or the nerds, or the "bad boys," or even those who had no interest in school, whatsoever. I wished I could have explained it, so those students would interact in class discussions, and get excited about the subject, and get more out of the lessons. As such, I felt well-prepared to be a teacher.

Unfortunately, both my parents, and several aunts and uncles, as well as three adults on our block were teachers, and they were all very strict, formal, permanently serious, and quiet. They rarely smiled, their mouths habitually pursed in thought or disapproval. Whereas, I had an out-going, loud, and sunny disposition, so I thought that I was way "too different" from them, as I liked to laugh, and sing, and dance, wear bright colors, and be creative, which I felt didn't go hand-in-hand with the role of an educator— judging from my role models. I felt that I wouldn't be accepted as a teacher, as my attitude appeared to be so different from other teachers. Basically, I was a right-brained person trying to fit into a left-brained world. So, because it was my groundless observation that *all* teachers acted in the same manner, I put my passion on hold.

As a senior in high school (1957), I had my life all planned out: I was to sign a dancing contract shortly after graduation, as I had been dancing on the stage for 15 years, since I was two-years-old. An older girlfriend was already on the dancing circuit, and I was to follow in her footsteps, on tour.

That Christmas, our parents threw a party, that neither my brother, nor I, knew anything about. As we were leaving for our separate dates that night, guests began arriving early. We were absolutely dumbfounded, as our parents had never hosted a party before (or since). They didn't even go to parties! They only rarely interacted with neighbors. We watched in total amazement, as many bottles of liquor were being carried through the door.

Now we had been raised with a teetotal mindset (no drinking, no smoking, no gambling, no swearing, no carousing, no drugs, no nonsense, and such). Total abstinence. Our lives were reminiscent of the later 1982 *Goody Two Shoes* song, by Adam Ant, with the lyric refrain: "Don't drink, don't smoke, what do you do?", to which I would always shout, "Not much!"

So my brother and I decided to stick around for a bit, and watch through the windows. We were absolutely fascinated to see the teachers—strangers from two districts, and two different grade levels—happily carrying on together: talking and laughing, and dancing, and obviously having a grand time. A smaller group was huddled around the piano in the dining room, singing Christmas carols at the top of their lungs, when for some reason, mother wanted it moved to the living room. So the piano player kept banging away on keys, as several burly men picked up the piano, and the crowd of carolers moved as one, into the next room, while neither the music nor song skipped a beat. I was thunderstruck!

As we left our window-watching perches, I had reached my turning-point. My whole life changed in an instant. Teacher could have *fun*! They could act silly, shout, be creative—and even *drink* and *smoke*! What a shocker! Teachers could actually have FUN! (Not that I would ever act silly or drink or smoke, but it was the *idea* that I couldn't if I wanted to; it was a matter of freedom of choice, and too many implied rules.)

I immediately scrapped my dancing plans, and went on to the university, and earned several degrees. And then taught for *fifty* years! (I retired for a whole 14 months, couldn't take it anymore, and returned to teaching.) I find it remarkable, that by observing that one unexpected party, my life was profoundly altered. It staggers the imagination.

"We're constantly affected by our experiences of life, and our experiences change our personality, our world-view, and our behaviors," says Thom Hartmann, in *The Prophet's Way*. According to Dr. Mark Thurston, in *Synchronicity as Spiritual Guidance*, Synchronicity " . . . brings about *processes of change at profound levels*." A synchronistic event very often becomes a turning point of one's life, as the above incident did for me. "Synchronistic opportunities often appear when we need them most," states Hopcke. "Whenever there are transitions to be made . . . synchronistic events very often play an important and sometimes decisive role."

And Dr. Richard A. Heckler, in his book *Crossings*, says that " . . . the unexpected need not be wildly dramatic to be transformative," which was certainly true in my case. Indeed, it is said that intense synchronicity meanings are often found in the smallest, seemingly insignificant details of everyday life. Standing outside, and watching the Christmas party through the windows, fairly shook the foundation of my life. The situation became a catalyst for deep change, for both my brother and me. And I made a powerful decision on the spot. I felt fundamentally changed, like my basic energy had shifted. All of my adult role models clearly showed that Learning Was Serious; enjoyment was not on the agenda. Whereas my attitude differed, maintaining that Learning Was Fun! Then I realized that teaching wasn't an either/or situation. Teaching and learning could be both serious and fun together, and, as such, I could and would become a teacher! Thurston adds: "If we recognize something meaningful in synchronistic events, it's up to us to do something with the insight that comes. We're challenged to . . . put the wisdom . . . into action." And, as a footnote to the above story, Richo adds: "Synchronicity happens so that we can advance toward our destiny."

EYE-OPENER

During the late sixties and early seventies, I was totally enmeshed in all the "new" metaphysical subjects, that are so prevalent in the general public nowadays. Very few books were written about such topics back then, and those that were were hard to find, so I had a really difficult time doing personal research. But I persevered. I found such subjects to be so exciting that I gave speeches about them to various groups, to share my newfound knowledge. (I was a teacher, after all.)

I was asked by the head of one group, if I would give a talk at the next month's meeting. I was slated to be the first speaker, and then, after the break, a special guest professor from New York City was going to give the major presentation. (New York City was about as far as you could get from California! Of course, I was thrilled to be the warm-up speaker! I couldn't wait to hear the pearls of wisdom from a real professor from afar!)

When I asked about the topic, I was told that I could speak on any subject.

"Any subject?" I reiterated. "But . . ."

"ANY SUBJECT!" she forcefully interrupted. So. Wow! Okay, I thought.

What to choose, what to choose? Everything was so fascinating to me, it would be a tough choice. At length, after a couple of days of indecision, I finally chose to present on a brand new word that I had just become acquainted with: Synchronicity.

When the date rolled around, I was ready: I had my stories, facts, and charts prepared. The audience was thoroughly engaged in my presentation. The material was all so new to them, that the resulting interactive question and answer period went way beyond our allotted time limit. Then we broke for our shared meal, with many happily discussing the topic, as we ate. When everyone was assembled again for the main event, the guest speaker was introduced with much fanfare and applause. He stood up, and powerfully barked, "My subject was to be Synchronicity, and SHE (jabbing his finger at me) said it much better than I ever could!" And he promptly sat down. He was NOT a happy camper. But as the shock wore off, the synchronicity of the situation was not lost on the audience, as everyone erupted into laughter, and excited chattering. *What fun!*

Years later, I, too, became a professor, and was invited to speak to various clubs and organizations, and at conferences, conventions, and for various school districts in different states.

HIGH FLYIN'

I was upset. After a two-week stay in the hospital, Jay, my six-month-old son, was scheduled for release that morning. But his temperature had elevated *one* degree, and the doctor decided to keep him an extra day, just to be on the safe side. I couldn't believe that *one* little degree was cause for such concern, and I was unhappy about it, in the extreme. In fact, I was as mad as a wet hen. I missed Jay.

Nursing heart-sick feelings, I was driving home on the freeway at a very fast clip. The traffic was lighter than usual, and I was traveling a number of car lengths behind a large moving van, with an open back door. I wondered if the company boss knew that a motorboat was being hauled therein. I highly doubted it. I figured that the workers had already delivered furniture early that morning, and on the QT were moving the privately-owned motorboat, without their boss's knowledge or consent.

I no more than considered that scenario, when the boat took flight out of the back of the moving van, sailing straight for me. I began swerving back and forth across the wide open lanes, trying to avoid the boat, while leaning on my horn at the same time, in an effort to alert the drivers behind me. The boat hit the pavement, with sparks flying, as it bounced erratically, then skidded over to the middle divider, ricocheted off the cement wall, and then flew in an arc back across three lanes, for a perfect crash landing on the hood of my car. It then bounced over the top of my car, and proceeded on its way in bumper car fashion, back down the freeway, damaging vehicles left, right, and center. Later, when the California Highway Patrol finally arrived (this was long before cell phones), there was a scraggly line of ten or so vehicles stretched along the side of the freeway—with various amounts of damage—alongside the many freaked out drivers. It took a long time getting home. Few people believed me, when I said, "A boat fell on top of my car on the freeway."

I was so thankful, and relieved that my son *hadn't* been released from the hospital that morning. The elevation of a mere one degree temperature may have saved his life. (This happened at a time before seatbelts and children's car seats were mandated, and Jay would, most likely, have violently landed on the floorboards, and rolled around, from pillar to post.)

I have always wondered what happened to the two workers that were driving the van. Did they lose their jobs? Did they have to pay restitution? Did the insurance cover the cost of all the cars? And I have pondered, as well, about just how much damage was caused, by not taking the time to tie down the boat, or simply close the moving van's backdoor.

"All is not necessarily what it seems to be at first blush," writes Hopcke, "and that the significance of what occurs may only be obvious later on." Heckler agrees: " . . . the most important events of our lives are little understood at first." And Richo chimes in with, " Synchronicity is found in an event that seems meaningless when it happens but later shows itself to be of utmost significance." Although the timing was a negative for me, it became clear that it was that very delay—that miniscule one degree— that led to a positive outcome. "The value of any experience, whether it seems positive or negative at the time, is best judged not by its drama, but by its fruits," so say Dan Millman and Doug Childers, in their *Bridge Between Worlds*.

And, Trish and Rob MacGregor say, in their Synchronicity blog (synchrosecrets.com), "Synchronicities multiply during periods of transition—a move, a marriage or divorce, a career change, a change in employment, or financial status, a birth, or a death." When unexpected, undesirable, or uncontrollable fateful detours come into your life, understand that all is not lost. (An old proverb says: Take it as a blessing, or take it as a test; whatever happens, happens for the best.) Later, when you stand back from the negative experience, and examine the bigger picture, you can see the positive; you can see the blessing. As Richo shares, " . . . a painful loss leads eventually to a surprisingly positive outcome." Like the old Chinese Zen "Bad Luck, Good Luck, Who Knows?" story, I have my own:

BAD LUCK/GOOD LUCK

I taught school in the daytime, and moonlighted as a waitress in the evenings, and on weekends. On the particular night in question, the Bob's Big Boy restaurant was packed, as usual, so servers were working in a whirlwind of activity.

I came out of the swinging kitchen doors, holding a tray aloft, carrying three bowls of hot bean soup. Unfortunately, the floor area in front of the doors, had just been mopped, and no one had been notified. My foot slid on the slippery surface, and I couldn't maintain my balance. And I went flying. Down I went, with the metal tray and broken pottery crashing all over the place, as hot soup splashed all over me. My white blouse turned instantly brown. Every person froze, as they witnessed the noise and the mess. It was one of those moments, I suppose, when everyone hoped someone else would do something about the situation. Talk about BAD luck!

Only one person leaped to my aid. Suddenly, as I opened my eyes, there was the most handsome man, staring into my face. He quickly introduced himself, saying that he worked in a hospital, and he was there to help me. So he gingerly pulled me up into a sitting position, and then helped me stand. The onlookers clapped, as he slowly led me through the swinging kitchen doors, and into the break room.

That unusual chance meeting, on the floor of the restaurant, turned into marriage. And we have been together for 49 years. Talk about GOOD luck!

All of which makes us consider the quote by Walsch: "It is a great truth that sometimes what we have called the biggest tragedy of our lives turns out to be he greatest gift we have ever received."

Jean Shinoda Bolen, M.D., discusses "accidental" remarkable connections, in her book, *The Tao of Psychology: Synchronicity and the Self*: "Synchronicity can pave the way for people coming together. By unraveling the circumstances through which two people meet to enter a *significant* relationship, the delicate unseen hand of fate, destiny, or synchronicity . . . can be discerned."

"Synchronicity is the surprise that something unplanned or unwanted suddenly fits." Synchronicity occurrences can be "life-affecting, destiny-promoting, and spiritually encouraging," says Richo.

BLUE

There was a new reality TV series, *Gold Rush*, that debuted on December 3rd, 2010. It was about four guys that take off for Alaska, to look for gold. The story behind the story is about my brother's dog, an Australian Shepherd, named

Blue. Terry owned 80 acres on top of a mountain in Oregon, which included a tree farm. Blue had the run of the property, played with Terry's seven children as they grew up, and was constantly chasing off the wild animals that lived in the area. Blue always barked at the airplanes that flew overhead. He had no fear whatsoever.

Being a globetrotter, Terry was constantly away for long periods of time. After his wife died, one of his daughters was left to live on the property, and run the tree farm. Then she got married, and for several valid reasons, couldn't oversee the farm anymore. So she closed up shop, and gave Blue away. She gave Blue to a man who was a sometime actor, who owned a large property with an airstrip. It was the perfect placement for Blue, as he had plenty of room to run and play and chase other wild animals, and bark at the planes. It was a good match. When Terry returned home, he was devastated by the loss of Blue, of course, but recognized that it was the best solution.

Fast forward several years, and the actor got a part in the new *Gold Rush* series, and took Blue with him to Alaska. During a two-week period prior to filming, the cast and crew needed to get to know each other, as well as get acquainted with the conditions and terrain. During this period, another of Terry's daughters flew to the campsite, as her husband had a client who was one of the actors. Can you guess which one?

When she got to the campsite, and was talking with some of the people— all strangers—she saw Blue in the distance, loping towards them, and they instantly recognized each other. Hence, the classic reuniting scene of them running towards each other, with her shouting and crying, and Blue barking joyfully. They collided in a giant hug, and rolled around in the grass together, as a camera recorded this unexpected event.

Later, one night, as the men had retired in their tents, and were deep asleep, they heard crashing, barking, and growling sounds. When they staggered out of their tents, they saw Blue chasing off a huge bear. They all realized that if Blue hadn't been there to watch over them, they may not have lived to tell about it. The four men bonded so thoroughly with Blue, that they insisted that Blue be in the show. And he was. Every now and then, throughout the series, viewers could see Blue trotting to and fro, in the background. It was said that Blue had become a favorite of all involved in the production, and there were rumors that he was getting his own show. *How fun is that?*

Sometimes, situations are so hectic, with so many distractions going on, you don't even realize that a coincidence or synchronicity situation has just happened, in the midst of the all the turmoil. Later, after the event, when you have time to calm down and consider the experience, the realization takes hold. Another case in point:

FIRST DAY

I should have known. Certainly, everyone had warned me. Friends and colleagues alike had rushed to tell me their own brand of "horror" stories about my new inner city school assignment. True, it was the most infamous school in our district, disaffectionately called "Looney Tunes"—but, always the optimist, I thought that things would be different for me.

I felt prepared. After all, I had *fifteen* years of excellent teaching experience, a background steeped in Educational Psychology, and a reputation for successfully handling "problem" children. *This*, after all, was my bailiwick. Furthermore, I had read everything available concerning inner city and ghetto life, and entered each day with my sleeves rolled up, metaphorically speaking. I assumed, therefore, in semi-divine arrogance, that *nothing* would come as a shock to me in my new teaching assignment. Thus armed, I looked forward to the challenge it presented. In other words, I had a bad case of Great Expectations. I should have known.

My first day was not to be believed. I was rather disturbed by having to wade through what seemed to be tons of litter (it looked like a SCUD hit!), to find new graffiti on my outside door, and fresh bullet holes in my class windows—a visual experience that I did not wish to have at that hour of the morning. (To one like myself who plows every bit of money I earn into beautifying my surroundings, this did not represent an auspicious beginning.)

This must be the place, I thought irreverently. I suppose I was showing an elitist attitude, but it *was* a bit of culture shock. The bad news to greet me was that the clocks weren't working, the bells were all off schedule, and the students couldn't use the bathrooms because *the walls were being painted.*

The children all looked so small as they came through the door. There also seemed to be more than the usual tears and hanging onto mothers' legs, but they settled down quickly enough. I noticed that some of their chins seemed to be resting on desktops. Questions about diet and physical examinations kept darting through my mind, as I greeted the youngsters. However, knowing that my first reaction to new third graders is always regarding size, I disregarded my doubts.

Indeed, there is a running joke in my household about how I always come home on the first day of each school year and wail, "But they're so *little!*" It has happened for so many years that my family expects this reaction, and enjoys parroting my conditioned response. Even with this memory uppermost in my mind, I *still* thought these children were too small.

As I spoke to the pupils, I got very little feedback other than wide-eyed stares. Not one normal third grade response did I get. They seemed *afraid* of me. Well, this is certainly new, I thought. Perhaps they've just never seen such a bombastic teacher before, I reasoned. After all, it takes a while for children to adjust to various teaching styles, I further cautioned myself.

My inner dialogue was interrupted by the voice of a teenager, as he led a tiny child through the door. "Sherry, whatever are you doing *here*? I'm delighted to see you!" After I got over the initial shock of being called by my first name in front of my new students, I whirled around to meet a sixteen-year-old runaway (the son of a teacher friend from my former school). We chatted for a few minutes—while I learned that he was a live-in babysitter for a local family—as he guided his young charge to a seat, while I kept a worried eye scanning my dwarfs. Added to my classroom concerns, I was now disturbed as to how I could convey the knowledge of this young person's safety and well-being to his mother, while, at the same time, not betraying his confidence.

"I didn't know you switched to first grade," he continued. "When did you make that decision?"

"I didn't! You must have the wrong room," I explained, as the light was beginning to dawn.

"No," he said. "See here," as he pointed to a room assignment card. There in black and white was the answer: the children *were* too small, being only six years old. When asked if they were first graders, the youngsters silently nodded their heads up and down. No wonder they seemed so frightened. I made a mental note to trust my instincts.

Not being able to leave the room myself, and having no working telephone, I sent all the children to the office with the few remaining parents, while I waited for my third graders to arrive. They didn't.

It seemed that all of my prospective pupils were in a collective mood to be somewhere else. So, when they had arrived at Room 11—the room assigned to them on their last year's report card— they found the door locked and the room dark, which gave them all the excuse they needed. This meant, they decided, that they didn't have to attend school. So some ran off to the playground, some went to the park across the street, and others drifted back to their own neighborhoods.

When the office finally figured out what had happened, several members of the staff had to go round up my students, and head them toward Room 14. The room was in a constant state of disruption and confusion; every time I started to say something, the door would fling wide open, and in would troop two or three more pupils—cocky and defiant—that everyone felt obliged to greet verbally.

"Oh, *no*! Look who's here!"

"Oooooh! He think he so BAD!"

"I be gonna *beat yore ass*!"

I'd seen happier faces on poison bottles. Needless to say, the rest of the day was spent in the same manner (only worse). Not only didn't they like one another, they didn't like *me* either. I was received with something less than enthusiasm, and felt as welcome as a wasp. The group—somewhat akin to a Greek chorus—demanded to know: (1) why I wasn't black, and (2) why I wasn't male.

These questions rather knocked me off my stride, as I was used to students *begging* to get into my class, as well as parents pressuring the office to get their children enrolled in my room. What a blow to my ego! I could feel my smile begin to set like a pan of fudge. It was my considered opinion that these misfits were the nastiest little brats I had ever had the misfortune to see. We were definitely in polarized positions. What a horrible predicament! Yet, I was determined to make all these noxious relationships work. It was clear to me that all these students needed unconditional acceptance, affection, and attention. I should have known.

After complaining to my husband about the truly unbelievable events of my

first day, an overwhelming feeling of
frustration descended upon me, when I
realized that I had yet to call my teacher
friend, to inform her that her missing
son was alive and well, and had a job.

Sometimes it's mind-blowing to consider the
odds of a situation. The *timing* of our classroom
meeting was of crucial significance. This was the
only morning in which this mismatch could have
occurred. *Ever.* In this synchronistic experience, I
could never have even accidently bumped into
them, at any other time, because the first grade
classrooms were housed in an entirely different
building, quite a distance away, on the opposite
side of the campus. And the first grade schedule
was different from the third grade schedule, so
our recesses and lunch periods were different,
and we had different playgrounds. Plus, the first
graders left school earlier than the third graders.
I was simply the conduit of information, but that
message had great *meaning* for both involved. My
friend and her son soon connected, patched up
their differences, and he was back in his family's
good graces. (Years later, I ended up writing my
first book about this particular third grade class,
and their wild and wooly, off-the-wall antics: *Into
the Hornet's Nest: An Incredible Look at Life in an
Inner City School*. It sold more books than all of
the rest of my books put together, and is now out
of print.)

ASTONISHED

When my *Autism ABC* book was newly published (2009), I sent copies to family, friends, neighbors, and anyone who had someone with autism in their families. Oddly, strangers began to send me money, along with notes to keep the autism awareness moving. So I would check the addresses of those individuals, and would place copies of the book in their closest neighborhood libraries. One man, who lived in Vacaville (*where the heck was that?*) also sent me money. When I checked for the closest library, all I found were three county libraries for that whole major farming area. So I sent several copies each, to all three libraries, and forgot all about it, in the hustle and bustle of daily life.

One day, a young neighbor from the next block (about third grade), brought a visitor from Northern California (about fifth grade) over to meet me. I have a number of unusual paintings, plants, books, and colorful stones, crystals, and geodes in each and every room, so children always find something that interests them. When they went into my library, the newcomer picked up a copy of *Autism ABC*, and happily announced, "Oh, I read this book!"

And I slowly shook my head, saying, "No, I'm afraid not. This book has only been out for a short while, and it has only been placed locally. So you must have read a similar book." We ended up arguing with each other. She finally told me that she and her girlfriend had gone to the library together, and she had checked out this book, and both read it together—because her friend has a little brother with autism. Then she told me what the book was all about. The impact was immediate: I was flabbergasted, realizing that they had found the book in one of those Northern California County Libraries. And I quickly apologized. Needless to say, I was thrilled with the news that *Autism ABC* was actually being put to good use!

To sum up: "A synchronicity can serve as guidance, warning, affirmation, creative inspiration, and/or as individuation and psychological growth. It can offer a glimpse into your future, and cause you to feel that you are on the right track, in the groove, exactly where you're supposed to be," so say the married writing team, Trish and Rob

MacGregor, in *The Seven Secrets of Synchronicity.* And Hopcke adds: "In all synchronicities, what is important is . . . the emotional impact they had on the people involved."

"Heavenly messages do not always come to us in heavenly packages or through heavenly experiences, the way we expect them to," explains Walsh. "They can be delivered in hot rock songs. Or twenty-year-old movie titles. Or widely popular, if improbable, books." Sometimes, it's the simple things, like reading a book, in which the timing and the meaning can promote a small synchronicity experience within you. This has happened to me on many occasions. As Gaulden points out, "Sports entertain for a night; a book can touch the world for years and years." And Pearl and Ponzlov said, "Often the synchronicity between what comes up in the book, and what come up in my life that day is awe-inspiring, presenting me with just the answers I didn't even know I was looking for."

More than mere coincidence, the presence of synchronicities in our lives may show that life has an incredible sense of meaning and purpose.
—Christiane Northrup, M.D.

INTUITION

Intuition is a perception,
of seeing, or hearing, or feeling,
rather than thinking.

—Mona Lisa Schulz, M.D., Ph.D.

INTUITION

The only real valuable thing is intuition.
—Albert Einstein

Many people don't believe in intuition, others distrust it entirely, while some believe in intuition, but don't think they have it. Yet many, like Laura Day in her book, *Practical Intuition*, tell us that your intuition plays a role in *every decision* you make.

Various dictionaries tell us that: Intuition is understanding something immediately, without the need for conscious reasoning; a direct perception of truth or fact, without rational thought or factual information; a gut reaction, and immediate response without forethought; an instinctive feeling; a quick and ready insight; you just *know*, without knowing how you know.

As in the words of Einstein, "I believe in intuition and inspiration . . . I sometimes FEEL that I am right. I do not KNOW that I am." He also said, "There comes a leap in consciousness, call it intuition, if you will, and the solution comes to you, and you don't know how or why." Or, as Mona Lisa Schultz, M.D., Ph.D., says, in *Awakening Intuition*, "Intuition occurs when we directly perceive facts outside the range of the usual five senses and independently of any reasoning process." And Laura Day agrees, "Intuition simply knows. Instantly. Where reason plods, intuition proceeds in flashes. Intuition gets glimpses of reality in bits and pieces, usually in symbols."

To paraphrase Neale Donald Walsch, on his "Awakening Intuition" and "I Believe God Wants You to Know" websites: Intuition is not a gift that some have and others cannot attain. . . It is not a question of whether you *have* it, but whether you are *using* it. Many have learned the hard way not to ignore even unsupported intuitions. Those individuals who experience coincidences, and find them to be intriguing, important and useful, also score high on intuition, states Beitman, M.D. Burnham agrees, reporting on a study of 500 subjects, in which 89 percent of the women and 72 percent of the men, experienced gut feelings about people or events, and 78 percent of skeptics had gut feelings in which their stomach was tied in knots. And C.G. Jung, M.D., suggests: ". . . put some trust in your intuition and follow your feeling . . ."

GUT REACTION

Two book agents who were a team, told me to *stop* writing *The Bogeyman: Stalking and its Aftermath*, and work on *Toxic Attention: Keeping Safe from Stalkers, Abusers, and Intruders* instead. I couldn't understand why, since *The Bogeyman* was my personal story (according to the FBI, I have the dubious honor of being the longest-stalked person in the nation—some 50+ years), whereas *Toxic Attention* was a companion self-help manual. And although I had major reservations about changing horses in midstream, I did what they suggested. After all, they were the experts, weren't they? So, I stopped work on the 6th chapter— when I was on a roll—to begin the new book. When I finally finished both books, I had lost track of the agents, and I never heard from them again. In the meantime, *The Bogeyman* then won The Book of the Year Award in the category of True Crime. I learned the hard way, to believe in myself, and pay close attention to my intuition.

If you tune into your intuition to determine meaning, you are tapping into your right-brain process. "Intuition is just another sense, like seeing or feeling or hearing . . . It is sometimes called the sixth sense," Schulz further explains. As W. Brugh Joy, M.D., related, "The wellspring that nourished my awareness was the knowing—the absolute *knowing*—that the course of action I was following was true to my soul." As Pearl said, "I knew. I mean I *knew*. I just didn't know how I knew." And Burnham agrees, "It's different from thinking, it's different from logic or analysis . . . It's a knowing without knowing." Steve Jobs called intuition "more powerful than intellect."

Day emphatically states that ". . . your intuition is first and foremost a survival tool." I can testify to that:

DANGEROUS STRANGER

When I was six years old, an elderly man tried to kidnap me from a department store. He kept following me around, talking to me, and making me feel uncomfortable. He said he wanted to buy a set of China for his sick wife, and didn't know what pattern to choose. He asked me to choose it for her. The housewares section was way in the back of the store, in an unlighted area where no one was, with one open outside door to an alley. Even though I was only in the second grade, I knew that a grown man wouldn't need a child to help him in that regard. At some subtle level, I felt threatened in a way that I didn't understand, and I didn't know how to deal with him, without being disrespectful. But I knew in my bones that I would be in deep trouble, if I got anywhere near that open back door. The situation didn't *feel* right—dark and unpleasant—and I felt small and vulnerable, which was a first for me. So I just pointed to the first pattern I saw, saying, "I choose that one!" and turned around and fled into the sizable crowd, that was upfront choosing valentines. No one paid any attention to me, as I ran inside the clerks' counter, and hid, as he came looking for me. I felt vaguely ashamed at being so frightened, and not knowing why. Remembering that situation always gives me the creeps. I wasn't sure what might have happened, or why it was danger that I sensed. I had no words for my experience, nor did I know what to complain about, and therefore, told no one. Even though I was raised to respect adults, and follow their directions, my intuition told me to get away from that man, as fast as possible. And I did. Parents and teachers didn't talk about predators in those days.

"There are moments . . . when our snap judgments and first impressions can offer a much better means of making sense of the world," Malcolm Gladwell, says in *Blink: The Power of Thinking Without Thinking*. Adding, "There can be as much value in the blink of an eye as in months of rational analysis." Indeed, my unconscious was scanning the room, sifting through possibilities, and processing every subtle, fleeting clue (facial expression, smile, eye contact, tone of voice, story). This flash of insight gave me the incentive to make a decisive, rapid-fire decision, under high pressure and with limited information. I immediately sized-up the situation—trouble!—and acted. Gladwell goes on to say, "Every waking minute that we are in the presence of someone, we come up with a constant stream of predictions and inferences about what that person is thinking and feeling." He continues: "As human beings, we are capable of extraordinary leaps of insight and instinct." Even at the young age of six.

"Intuitive hits are sudden, immediate, and unexpected ideas," offers Schulz. "Intuitive insights involve emotion. They're hard to describe in words." And, according to Dan Millman, in his *Everyday Enlightenment*, "Intuitive decisions tend to be more aligned with our own subconscious mission and destiny." With regard to medical, business, and all relationship matters, do your research, get good advice, and then do what *feels* intuitively right.

DECISION

I spent a great deal of time, researching the various university doctoral programs. At that time, no California universities held evening, weekends, or summer programs, for teachers, which meant that one would have to take a leave of absence, which was frowned upon by districts. So I had to look to other states. I agitated, fumed, and fussed over the best programs available. There were positives and negatives involved. Then, on the last possible day to meet a particular application deadline, I had a gut feeling; a calm sense of *knowing*, that I needed to get my application in the mail, that particular day. So I filled out the proper forms, wrote my mission statement, and had my photo taken. Then I stood in line at the post office, to send my package by Priority Mail. I felt *good* about my decision, without a care in the world. I wasn't worried in the least, thinking that the university would happily take my money. As a result, I didn't apply to other universities. (*What did I know?*) Then the testing began. Serious business. I had no idea that 5,000 other people, worldwide, had applied, to be in the four-year doctoral program, which was limited to 42 students (only seven of which were women!). The selection took place over a number of months, in which the final 100 applicants met altogether in a meeting hall, with the leaders of the program. And we all kind of milled around, and introduced ourselves, and spoke to each other, in this totally unstructured "getting-to-know-you" event. I had no clue that this was the final count-down. And I didn't even find out about the odds of making the cut, until I was halfway through the program. And I freaked out! (I got all nervous, and shaky, and my stomach started doing flips-flops, and I felt like I needed to throw up—long after the fact.) I would have been a basket case during the tests and interviews, had I known beforehand. Thank goodness my intuition had taken over.

"Intuition is a natural state, like breathing, and the only time you inhibit it is by addiction to drugs or alcohol, mind-altering substances intended to induce power, but which instead, disrupt the wisdom of the mind," states Burnham. Good to know. Intuition gives you a whole new perspective, as Schulz poetically puts it: "Intuition helps you to look beyond the dominating weeds, to search for ways to make the flowers grow."

Intuition is a valuable tool for sign interpretation. Often, your intuition comes into play during the translation of the message, and you don't even realize it. "Every time you follow your intuition, your personal vibration intensifies," says Denise Linn, in *The Secret Language of Signs*, adding,

". . . the more you follow your intuition, the more balanced and in tune you will be." Redfield says almost exactly the same thing: "Every time we follow an intuition and some mysterious encounter leads us forward, our personal vibration increases." And Millman says, "Trusting your instinct and intuition is a way of listening to your highest wisdom." I agree with all of them, since I am alive today, as the direct response of paying attention to my intuition. I speak from experience.

> *Trust your intuition to the end,*
> *though you can render no reason.*
> —Ralph Waldo Emerson

DREAMS

*A dream is the theater where
the dreamer is at once,
scene, actor, prompter,
stage manager, author,
and critic.*

—Carl G. Jung, M.D.

DREAMS

DREAMS

A dream is like a
personal document,
a letter to oneself.
—Calvin Hall, Ph.D., dream research pioneer

Some people think that dreams are just so much brain-lint; a confusion of nonsensical images. Other people agree with Watkins, who says that " . . . dream symbols can represent endless layers of meaning and association." Day suggests that dreams " . . . appear to operate as a kind of down-loading system. Dreams focus on our awareness on things we've noticed throughout the day but haven't noted. They bring up to 'semiconsciousness' information necessary for our psychological well-being."

In fact, Freud maintained that: "Dreams are a conversation with oneself, a dialog of symbols and images that takes place between the unconscious and conscious levels of the mind." And Jung—the renowned psychiatrist and author—is best known as an explorer of human nature, the collective unconscious, and dreams, said that a dream should be regarded *seriously*, and it should be analyzed to see how it would fit into a person's conscious life.

According to Edgar Casey, anyone who can dream, and can remember the dream, is capable of learning from the dream, and is capable of adding conscious insight and behavior to the experience. "... there are four kinds of dream imagery: nonsense, literal, symbolic, and visionary," documented Dr. Harmon Hartzell Bro, in his book, *Edgar Casey On Dreams*. "But most dream content is symbolic, or 'emblematic.'" Casey insisted that, "Each person's way of dreaming is as individual as his fingerprint, " ... and in Casey's view, "Every dreamer has his own repertoire of personal symbols or emblems, loaded with shades of meaning displayed in dreams." Note that every symbol and every character in your dream is an aspect of yourself.

"Having different filters, none of us see or hear exactly the same world. We view the same objects but perceive different meanings," states Dan Millman. "The same words have different meanings for different people." I found that out for myself, when my *Imperfect Weddings are Best* was published. With over 250 examples of weddings that went awry, I agonized and worried that all of my relatives would be mad at me, for what I wrote about their weddings. I was astounded to find that *not one* person recognized the funny bloopers that I wrote about. They all had a different perspective, and a different story to tell. It blew me in the weeds, and I was sooooo thankful.

Your dreams can be a cornucopia of information, containing valuable signs and messages. They often " . . . highlight issues in need of attention, resolution, or closure," say Phyllis R. Koch-Sheras, Ph.D., Amy Lemley, and Peter L. Sheras, Ph.D, authors of *The Dream Sourcebook & Journal*.

Your dreams can be predictive. Abraham Lincoln believed that *all* dreams have significance. Indeed, he had a prophetic dream about his own assassination. Likewise, Sugar Ray Robinson had a prophetic dream the night before he was to fight Jimmy Doyle, in 1947. He dreamed he killed his opponent with a left hook. He was so shaken upon awakening, that he said he wouldn't fight Doyle. The promoters brought in a Catholic priest to assure Robinson that his fears were unfounded. As the dream forewarned, however, in the eighth round, Sugar Ray hit Doyle with a left hook, so hard that he was carried off the ring on a stretcher, and he died the next day. (Check out other such synchronicity stories at Trish and Rob MacGregor's synchronicity blog at: blog.synchrosecrets.com)

And, too, dreams can be prescient, extrasensory, and psychic. Your dreams are among your greatest messengers. Paying attention to your dreams is " . . . a way to get in touch with your mind's unconscious thinking processes," Burnham told the *Huffington Post*. Adding that, "Paying attention to your dreams is a way to get in touch with your mind's unconscious thinking processes." She went on to say that, "If you're attuned to your dreams, you can get a lot of information about how to live your life." Consider such dreams to be signals or messages. Understand that there is no right or wrong way to sort out the symbolism involved in your dreams. You are the judge and the final authority. And whenever you remember your dreams, they need to be used in some way, if at all possible. Act upon the dreams you recall.

Your dreams start preparing you for what life will give you, weeks, months, years, and even decades in the future, says Robert Moss, in *The Three "Only" Things*. Both scientists and mathematicians have dreamed specific answers to their problems; Winston Churchill at 14, dreamed that one day he would lead the country, save the capital, and the empire; many authors, like Steven King and Richard Bach, say they have received plot lines from their dreams; and music and song lyrics have come via dreams (Paul McCarthy dreamed his song, "Yesterday" from the Beatles album HELP! in 1965, which The Guinness Book of Records holds that over 3000 versions were recorded, and performed over seven million times in the 20th century alone, while listeners on the BBC Radio 2 voted it the best song of the 20th century, and it was voted the #1 Pop song of all times by MTV and the Rolling Stone Magazine.) We should all be so lucky with our dreams.

Dreams are often synchronistic events. They show us things that we may prefer not to think about, but *need* to think about, Moss says. "Dreams may relate both to a literal phenomenon *and* to an emotional or symbolic condition." And the scarier the dream, the more urgent the need to figure it out, and do what needs to be done. Dreams can save your life. I know this from personal experience. Moreover, as Hopcke points out, when people resist or ignore dream messages, their dreams become more explicit. He likens such dreams to fairy tales, in which it takes three tries to get things right. Unfortunately for me, it took much, much longer, as I refused to believe the messages. (The following example is reprinted from my third book, *The Bogeyman: Stalking and its Aftermath*, pp. 52-55. Nine years later—on 12/12/12—my story became the premier episode on the Investigation Discovery channel, for the *Someone's Watching* series. I was told that it became their most popular rerun.)

THE WORMS CRAWL IN

And then there came a time when the Night Train chugged into my life, and my vaguely threatening anxiety dreams graduated into full blown nightmares. Heretofore, the dreams of my youth had been beautiful, life-enhancing experiences, from which I awakened renewed, refreshed, and revitalized. Now the creepy-crawly terrors of the night took hold, and I slid into the world of Hieronymous Bosch. Later, I dreamed a series of operatic dramas, including voice-overs, flashbacks, and fantasy sequences—two or three each night—in which I was murdered in the culminating scene. Each in a different manner. By Chuck, my husband. These dreams were brilliantly intense and gloomy, with accompanying sound effects, while the disturbing strains of Chopin's Opus no. 35 ("Marche Funebre") played solemnly in the background: Dum, dum, da dum, dum, dum, dum, da dum, da dum. It was all too gothically spooky.

Although each murder was creatively different from the next, the final scene was *always* the same. My coffin was slowly lowered into the ground, and after thumping to a stop, I could hear the dirt shoveled in on top of it: thud, thud, thud. Jolted wide-awake, freaked out and jittery, with my heart hammering wildly in my chest, a warped recording of "The Worms Crawl In" ominously scratched into my awareness. Of course, with 31 flavors of fear coursing through my mind, I was afraid to go back to sleep. It was most disturbing. *Wasn't it enough that my days were in shambles?* I continuously asked myself. As my existence seemed barren beforehand, it simply didn't seem fair to add nightmares o the mix.

So, now I had something new to stew about: *What was the message I was missing here? What was this repeated nudging from my neural wiring all about? What was the night-side of my brain trying to say?* I suddenly had a real interest. Never having been one to do things in moderation, I became a champion researcher. I plunged heavily into the subject of dreams, in a determined effort to scratch this mental itch. Like a junky on a binge, I absorbed every printed word I could find on the subject, reading dozens upon dozens of books and articles, in an attempt to understand my situation. (I collected 69 books on the subject, that are stacked one on top of the other, in a 7-foot high column, next to my bed, which I no longer bother with.) It was writ so large you could have read it from the Skylab, but I ignored the obvious, of course. I found many items of interest. The most useful for my immediate purposes were:

(1) Dreams tell us not only what we want or desire, but what we *need*, as well.

(2) Dreams involve showing what we may not be seeing: directing attention to whatever we are most in danger of ignoring, or rejecting, in our everyday affairs.

(3) When our outlook becomes too rigid or limited, dreams can give the other side of the picture.

(4) In a crisis, when our lives are threatened by outside circumstances, we will have the most vivid and meaningful dreams.

Aha! Eureka! Excelsior! And, because one dream often throws light on another, experts suggest that far more satisfactory results can be obtained by trying to interpret them in *groups*, rather than looking at each one in isolation. Realizing that I had a problem of not seeing the forest for the trees, I decided to start recording my dreams in a diary, which I maintained for seven years thereafter.

Consciously, I hadn't a clue as to what was going on, but luckily, instinct and intuition lent their guidance. Thank goodness I was picking up information subliminally, so I finally got the message: I was being sized up for a chalk outline.

Chuck was *literally* plotting my imminent death.

Then I started reconsidering all of the near misses, and the variety of unusual incidents, I had encountered over a number of months. For instance, Chuck would drive like a maniac, taking foolish chances, getting to within inches of creaming dogs and cats. Was he hoping to scare me to death via a heart attack? He would speed and stop, speed and stop, repeatedly slamming me into the dashboard. (This was in the days before seatbelts). He followed this with a series of deliberate near misses. He would aim at a telephone pole, street lamp, parked vehicle, tree, or whatever, driving as fast and as close as possible before jerking away at the last moment. Of course, the object in question was always on the *passenger* side. I just thought he was a *sicko*, playing chicken with inanimate objects, and didn't see a more sinister plot.

For a number of weeks, he worked at hoping to make me think I was losing my mind, but he couldn't pull it off. I wasn't going for it. He'd make statements out of the blue, apropos of nothing, as if we'd been in the middle of a long conversation, or having no relationship whatsoever to what we'd actually been discussing, acting like I couldn't remember what had just transpired. *Give me a break, Wacko*. He finally gave up that plan, since I couldn't be convinced.

One night, as I was getting out of the tub, always an intensely modest experience for me, he barged in and *unintentionally* bumped my radio into the bathwater. I was more concerned with the lack of privacy than the fact that I had just missed being electrocuted. My brakes were tampered with on another occasion. And so forth, and so on.

Taking another look at the string of bizarre *accidents*, and putting them altogether, the light finally dawned. *Duh*. One needn't be a member of Mensa to guess his intentions, but I'm obviously a slow learner. (Or I didn't want to admit the possibility.) As the cold breath of reality sank in, the background beat of a headache began, that rarely went away thereafter. I'd never been afraid of dying, but dying before my time, at the hands of another, was an entirely different matter. I realized that under the circumstances, caution was definitely in order from here on out.

At length, I accused him of planning to murder me. Breaking into a malevolent grin, Chuck happily answered in the affirmative, taunting me in exuberant glee, "A wife can't testify against her husband!" This sentence became a mantra to him. I heard that spousal privilege line, over and over again, delivered with undisguised hilarity. *"A wife can't testify against her husband!"* Those seven words were etched on the front of my mind like the carvings on Mount Rushmore.

According to Cayce, a gloomy outcome or low spirits at the end of a dream underscores a warning, whereas adventure or discovery or attractive locales at the end of a dream indicates a promise or good times.

Dreams are " . . . a way of keeping emotional balance, and releasing the suppressed difficulties in waking life," Linn tells us. "Bad dreams have the most important messages," says Redfield. Unfortunately, I found that out for myself. In Casey's view, "Any condition ever becoming reality is first dreamed." Yikes! "Compare the story of the dream to the story of your life," Redfield adds.

Through the decades, researchers and scientists have suggested that dreams are a problem-solving mechanism of the brain," says Schulz. "Dreams are like open windows through which we can focus and see images of our emotions . . . without the gauzy curtains, and distractions of life during the day getting in the way." What a beautiful way to explain it.

Did you know that more of your brain is awake when you're asleep, than when you are awake and conscious? Scientists tell us that when you're asleep, your whole brain lights up, like a dazzling chandelier, because it is free from interference from the outside world. And it can send you emotional information, showing what needs to be changed in your life. Casey maintained that, "The function of dreams was not alone to solve problems. It is to move the dreamer forward in his total life and growth . . . and awaken him to his full stature as a person." Since you spend a third of your life sleeping, and you dream more than a thousand dreams a year, make the most of it. Decipher your messages. Dream on!

Dreams prepare, announce, or warn
about situations long before they happen.
—Carl Jung, M.D.

COLOR

Each color is a specific signpost for you.
—Denise Linn

Color is a part of your everyday life. It is all around you. We see it all the time, but we take it for granted. Color is so important. It would be bleak and boring to live in a black and white world, like the old-time movies. Ted Andrews, author of the popular *Nature-Speak book*, tells us that the colors of plants, flowers, trees, and animals, "stir emotions and resonate subtly with our body and mind." "Color is one of the greater keys to the vocabulary of the dream world," explains Ann Ree Colton, in her *Watch Your Dreams*, "as color is the life within the symbol."

It is my observation that many Americans are *afraid* of color: beige clothes, beige furnishings, beige lives. (A lawyer friend jokes that everything in his life is beige, or a variation thereof: his turkey dinner with a roll, his file folders, his Post-it notes, his khaki pants, the couch, his cat, and so forth.) Don't succumb to the cultural pressure towards sameness. Beige is bland, impersonal, and anonymous. You are here to be colorful. Do everything with your eyes wide open. Allow yourself to be seen!

Color affects people's moods. Psychologists, artists, and interior designers, as well as those in marketing and advertising, understand how colors dramatically affect moods, feelings, and emotions. "Color is a powerful communication tool, which can be used to signal action, influence moods, and cause physiological reactions," states Kendra Cherry, on the Verywell.com website.

Most of us have no idea the impact color has on our lives. And this impact of the color in our environments is usually not a conscious observation. Warm colors (reds, oranges, yellows) are inviting, happy, and stimulating, whereas cool colors (blues, greens, purples) are relaxing, calming, and soothing.

"Your attitude is like a box of crayons that color your world. Constantly color your picture gray, and your picture will always be bleak. Try adding some bright colors to the picture by including humor, and your picture begins to lighten up," says Allen Klein. And Burchard agrees, saying "We choose the color of our own sky."

FAVORITE COLOR

One day, the second graders asked me about my favorite color. I said that I preferred orange, whereas my husband liked red, and therefore I had an orange

V.W. and he had a red V.W. I looked upon a sea of blank faces.

"What's a V.W.?" they wanted to know.

"Oh, it's a Bug!" I explained, thinking everyone had seen the Walt Disney movie, *Herbie the Love Bug.* Silence again. "What's a Bug?" they chorused. "A VeeDub." Nothing. "A Volkswagen!" Nada. Zip. Zilch.

Not until I took them outside and showed them, did they get the picture. The word *car* would have sufficed.

Mostly, we work with the eight basic colors—red, yellow, blue, green, orange, purple, black and brown—with gray and white thrown into the mix. (Although, in my youth, we were constantly told that white wasn't a color, it is now called "a color without color"). Or, if we are lucky enough, we can deal with the popular 64 colors in a Crayola box. We don't want to be bothered with the 150 hues that our eyes can recognize. Nor do we want to have to choose between the over 3,500 paint colors by Benjamin Moore. We would be simply overwhelmed with any more colors, as experts have estimated that there are anywhere from a low of 100,000, to 2.3 million, to 10 million colors (as edited by Glen Elert), or even 180 million colors that are said to exist, according to Pearl and Ponzlov. Yikes! Too many choices.

23 YEARS LATER

Today I spent time working on this "Colors" chapter, and decided to take a break. I began sifting through a stack of my research books, trying to decide if I could take a few back to my library room, so I wouldn't have so many taking up space in my computer room. As I flipped through one book, I came across the name James Redfield, and *The Celestine Prophecy*. And realized that I hadn't thought of that book in years (23, to be exact)! And I remembered that it had a rather unusual, dark color cover— either bluish-green or greenish-blue— so it might be easier to find, than others. Now being a well-known bookaholic, I have several thousand books in the house. Books are housed in each room, plus my library (three walls with floor to ceiling shelves). But I knew that if I actually still had it, the book would be in my heavily overstocked library, on the left side of the room, because that half holds all of my metaphysical and spiritual books. So I walked right in, almost to the far wall (which was peculiar in itself), and thought, *now where shall I start to look?* I first turned my head and saw, at eye level, on one of the corner shelves, what I thought to be a trace of that odd color. I immediately removed a large, tall, intricately carved candle, and pulled out the book, directly behind it! Good Golly Miss Molly! It didn't take me even a finger-snap of time to find it! I clasped it to my chest—in great joy—as I danced back into the living room. When I sat down, ripples went up and down my spine, a sure confirmation that this was important. Even though it was after midnight, I sat right down and read through all my faded yellow highlightings from all those many years ago, and found eight quotes, that I might be able to use. *How fun is that?*

ODD TIMING

And speaking of synchronicities, a week after writing the above, an old acquaintance called me from Big Bear, the mountain area to which she had settled. I hadn't connected with her for at least three years, or so. In the midst of our mile-a-minute conversation, and apropos of nothing, she suddenly asked if I had ever read *The Celestine Prophecy*, by James Redfield. Now how strange is that?!

The role of color in your life may be far more extensive, and important, than you are aware.

GRAY DAY

As any teacher can tell you, there are some children who are in class in body only, as there doesn't seem to be any activity going on inside their heads. Terrence was one such child, who always seemed to have a vacuum between his ears. Several school months had gone by, in which he seemed to have no connection whatsoever with what was going on in the classroom. I had to resist the impulse to knock on his noggin and ask, "Yoohoo! Are you in there?" Clearly, he had the brains of an oyster.

Whenever he contributed to class discussions, it was always some off-the-wall comment that was not even vaguely connected to the topic at hand. We had all come to expect this kind of behavior from him, and the class largely ignored his attempts to communicate. He was definitely marching to the tune of a different drummer.

One day, however, will live long in my memory. We had taken a field trip to Marineland, and on the bus ride home he had a heretofore unfamiliar look about him as he shared a starling discovery with me. "Ms. Meinberg! Ms. Meinberg!" Terrence yelled—when a lightbulb flashed over his head like a character in a cartoon strip—as he excitedly pointed out the window. "See how the sky is the same *color* as the Pacific Ocean!"

I just about died from shock, as he had actually merged two subjects (geography and art) into one understandable sentence. And, furthermore, his observation was correct, as the gray of the day was so pronounced that you couldn't find a line between the waves and the sky. (He had, previous to this moment, called the ocean "the big waters" and only recognized the sky as big, blue, and up high.)

I almost cried right there on the spot. The whole trip had been worth all the hassle involved, for just that *one sentence* alone. It was as if someone had flipped a switch on inside his head, as Terrence was always on target thereafter, and his subsequent learning was phenomenal. He had successfully broken out of his intellectual coma. You just never know what will turn a child "on."

Nature is filled with color. With over 250,000 species, the plant kingdom, (also known as the "green" kingdom)—grasses, plants, flowers, mosses, ferns, trees—is the second largest kingdom. It is filled with the most unique colorations, combinations, and variations.

And, the Rainforest internet site shows that color is extremely important throughout the animal kingdom (mammals, birds, insects, spiders, fish), as well. Camouflage allows creatures to blend in with their surroundings (lizards, goldenrod spiders, Australian tree frogs, flounders, octipi, and squid). Others go bold and bright to warn predators of their poisonous or venomous status (snakes, hornets). The Smashing Tops website, and the Wikipedia site show how some creatures change their colors to mimic other species (the golden tortoise beetle, stick bugs). While others use their vivid colors to attract sexual partners (peacocks, birds of paradise). Chameleons change colors to communicate, as well as to make themselves more attractive to mates. For some animals, the change comes quickly, for others it's seasonal. The Momtastic WebEcoist site clearly shows how some animals shift their coats in the winter (caribou, artic foxes, weasels, birds, rabbits) to blend with their surrounding environments. Others differ only slightly between shades, whereas some go from fully brown to white. Color is important to all living things.

In the same manner, as Jerry Cao explains on the creativebloq.com website, organizations use different colors in their logos, ads, store walls, signs, and websites. Each color is a conscious and deliberate choice depending upon the target *mood* they want to elicit.

Likewise, there is a link between clothing colors, accessory choices, and emotional states. People who are depressed often lose interest in how they look, and don't wish to draw attention to themselves, or stand out in a crowd. As Rheyanne Weaver tells us on the GoodTherapy.org website, studies show that wearing outfits of colors that evoke feelings of happiness, optimism, and energy will positively boost your mood. Give your clothing colors some thought, and get out of your doldrums.

Colors must fit together
as pieces in a puzzle
or cogs in a wheel.
—Hans Hofmann

The following short color compilation list is the result of various experts on the subject: Andrews, Cao, Colton, Linn, the MacGregors, Mascarenhas, and Upczak. Colors have psychological and cultural meanings, as well as your own personal associations. Use this list for dream interpretation, or to choose colors as you dress, or paint your walls, to represent the emotions you desire. Pick meanings that suit you best.

COLOR MEANINGS

Beige/Khaki – neutral, uninteresting, non-involving, uninspiring, indecisive, ordinary, dull, boring, bland, flat, stale, blah, ho-hum, impersonal, tedious, mundane, monotonous, anonymous, or enhances other colors, a powerful secondary choice

Black = powerful, elegant, sophisticated, grounding, quiet strength, protection, edgy, mystery, or unknown, indifferent, unaware, or obstruction, darkness, hidden thoughts, negative, secretiveness, mourning, confused, the shadow, depression, ominous, supernatural powers

Blue = serene, happiness, soothing, calmness serenity, tranquility, sensitivity, healing, peace, love, devotion, trustworthy, truthful ("true blue"), honesty kindness, spirituality, mystical perceptions, darker blues project professionalism, security, safety, or introversion, deep secrets, depression ("the blues"), loneliness, faultfinding

Bronze = lower subconscious

Brown = solid, stability, grounded, earthy, outdoorsy, sturdy, rustic, organic matter, common sense, security, practical, reliable, industrious, service, satisfaction

Gold = wealth, endurance, success, empires, kingdoms, reigns of power, confidence, courage, manifestation, creative thought, communication, enthusiasm, superiority, solar light or illumination, soul-power, soul-grace, soul-memory, divine intelligence, enlightenment

Gray = neutral, tired, lifeless, confusion, misunderstanding, detachment, aloofness, gloomy, despair, fear, foggy dreams, or when wearing gray professionally: good taste, formality, dignity, self respect

Green = health, youth, healing, renewal, abundant, growth, balance, harmony, new ideas, love, fertility, communication, social, natural, acceptance, abundance, prosperous, money, serenity, tranquility, the heart, peace, good luck

Lavender = spring, romance, love, mother consciousness, lover of tradition

Orange = optimism, expansiveness, new beginnings, social, fun, happy, playful, warm-hearted, tolerant, enthusiastic, self-motivating, energetic, stimulates creativity, productivity, optimism, energetic, expression, social, affection, warmth, sensuality, harmony, abundance, balance between the mind and emotions, health, vitality, time to act

Peach = happiness, balance, mellow, charming, disarming, courage, healing, or forlorn, despair, fear

Pink = love, devotion, purity, youth, innocence, joy of life, sweetness, tenderness, playfulness, softness, femininity, sensitivity, compassion, chastity, reverence, faith, or immature, fickleness

Purple = luxurious, elegance, mysterious, beautiful, romantic, first love, passionate, serenity, spiritual wisdom, psychic perceptions, power, telepathy, sensitivity, creativity, rules, regulations, tradition, the past, royalty, nobility, ceremony, mystery, spirituality, or pompousness, arrogance

Red =vibrant, important ("the red carpet"), full of life, attention getting, strong emotion, love, warmth, enthusiasm, excites, dynamic energy, spontaneity, passionate, sexuality, or intense, warning, stop, anger, danger, revenge

Silver = coins, wealth, courage, flexibility, versatility, or intuition, psychic awareness, or moonlight, magical, mystical, cool emotions

Turquoise = protection, strength, healing, wealth, good fortune, peace, communication, initiative, happy, relaxed, truth, creativity, wisdom, individual responsibility, self-reliance, independence, nobility, immortality

Violet — tenderness, selfless love, idealism, intuition, artistic endeavors, fulfillment, higher awareness, spirituality

White = good, cleanliness ("spotless"), purity, truth, openness, awareness, understanding, insightful, realization, positive thinking, the new, the beginning, divine protection, spiritual advancement, reverence, light, chastity, virginal, perfection, a happy, healthy nature, or cold, sterile, barren, stark

Yellow = happy, friendly, joyful, sunny disposition, intellect, learning, inquisitive, lighthearted, uplifting, communicative, increases fun, humor, lightness, happiness, enthusiastic, stimulates, vitalize, order, logic, legal documents, personal power, intellect, courage, confidence, personal power, or bright yellow is the color of warning signs and taxis

Note that different shades of each color also have distinct meanings. There are many meanings for the various shades of blue, gray, orange, and yellow, which are not included herein (such as: yellow, canary yellow, lemon, daffodil, sunflower, maize, mustard, goldenrod, citrine, chartreuse yellow, clear yellow, and golden yellow).

Understand, too, that muddy colors show a foggy outlook, stagnation, fearfulness, sickness, and refusing to face one's mixed emotions. Pale colors come across as weak, feeble, bland, unimpressive, depleted vitality, timidity, and meandering thoughts.

Zodiacal colors are said to influence the personality, as shown by Colton:

Aries — fiery orange
Taurus — emerald green
Gemini — indigo blue
Leo — golden peachy
Virgo — canary yellow
Libra — opalescent
Scorpio — crimson orange
Sagittarius — turquoise blue
Capricorn — ruby crimson
Aquarius — aquamarine blue
Pisces — violet

*I found that I could say things with color
and shapes that I couldn't say any other way—
things I had no words for.*
—Georgia O'Keeffe

SIGNS

*You'll drive yourself crazy if you
start trying to pry the meaning out of
every gust of wind or rain squall.
I'm not denying that there might actually
be a few signs that you don't want to miss.
Knowing the difference is the tricky part.*

—David Eddings

SIGNS

"Sign, sign, everywhere a sign
Blockin' out the scenery, breakin' my mind
Do this, don't do that, can't you read the sign?"
—Les Emmerson, songwriter for
Five Man Electrical Band (1970)

We get signs each and every day, in a million different ways. You see signage on a daily basis: For Sale, No Smoking, For Rent, No Trespassing, No Pets, Closed. And you see advertising signs on billboards, buses, taxis, blimps, and skywriting, not to mention, in newspapers, magazines, and on your computers.

In addition, you are always encircled by signs of another kind: the hidden dimensions of life. "Things are hitting us over the head all the time. But in our culture, we are trained not to see them," Day tells us. These are portents and omens in which all occurrences have meaning and significance for you, and you alone. "Signs are powerful indicators that can give you understanding about yourself and insight about direction in life," Linn tells us. A sign is any object, action, event, or pattern that conveys meaning. "The Universe talks to us continually. It sends messages through signs," says Marcoux, "The Universe sends signs to answer your questions."

There is a universal language, one with no spoken words involved (hunches, intuitions, gut reactions, guide-signs, symbols and dreams). This unspoken language also uses the echo effect—a repetition of events, ideas, and people, to make a point. Linn continues, "Fundamentally, signs have two functions. They serve as messengers of important information about your present circumstances and even about your future, and they act as reflections of where you are in your life." You can count on signs.

The Universe gives us messages all the time, in dramatic or subtle ways, showing us direction and guidance through the language of signs. Rushnell agrees, saying, " . . . the Universe has been erecting signposts—winking directly at you—all along your life's path." All you need to do is to be open: pay attention, identify the signs, and interpret them. He goes on to say that you need to "Yield to the signs. Along every highway are big signs and little signs. They all have meaning. You wouldn't accept or dismiss a road sign because of its size, would you?"

Unfortunately, most people don't pay attention to the signs, nor do they recognize them for what they are. We mostly pay attention to the hiccups, stumbling blocks, and bricks. "It's the bricks in life, the heartaches, the trials and troubles that get our attention," continues Marcoux, "The more accepting and open you become, the quicker the Universe's signs emerge. Be on the lookout for signs. "The more attention you give to looking for these signs, the more they will show up in your life."

If you need some guidance, ask. Ask the Universe. Ask for help. Ask for guidance, counsel, or advice. To paraphrase Walsch, your answer will come directly and immediately, although it may come in an unlikely or unexpected form. But it will come to you. Your only job will be not to ignore it, but to actively look for the answer.

Remember the promise: *Ask and it shall be given unto you*. Proactively solicit information. Set the intention that you will receive a sign. The more attention you give to looking for such signs, the more they will show up in your life. I'm always alert for SIGNS FROM THE UNIVERSE: a radio comment, TV ads, newspaper headlines, magazine quotes, songs, random overheard remarks, billboards, postcards, cloud formations, business cards, fortune cookies, skywriting, or through the unexpected appearance of an animal, object, or event. Watch for signs. "Understand that the manner in which you interpret a sign is less important than the meaning you derive from it," says Linn.

SALSA

The other day, I had lunch with my friend at a Mexican restaurant. I knew better, when I ate a bunch of salsa, because it doesn't always agree with me. But it sure was good, so I kept eating it. Alas, much later, on the way home, my stomach started gurgling and growling and churning. Big time. And I was suddenly in a race to get home to my bathroom in time. I lost. Yikes! And, adding insult to injury, the license plate on the car in front of me read: U IDIOT! *Can you believe*? I definitely won't pull that stunt ever again. Oh, woe is me. Lesson learned.

Sometimes the sign will be subtle. Sometimes the sign will jump out at you with its message, like a knock on the noggin.

BOOKS

In my twenties, when I would walk down the aisles of various bookstores, I might find a book on the floor, or a misplaced book, or a book would suddenly fall from a shelf, landing at my feet. When I would pick it up, my whole body would tingle and ripple. Knowing that this was a sign from the Universe—that the book had not come into my awareness by accident—I would buy it, as I knew it had a special message for me.

Unfortunately, now, as my second home is the *only* local bookstore available—Barnes & Noble—where I spend a great deal of time, and know the stock inside and out, and know when new titles are being shelved (Tuesdays), this experience doesn't happen to me anymore. And I miss such out-of-the-blue eureka moments. Signs can take you by surprise.

BLIMP

I was always beseeching the Universe for a sign, to tell me if readers were going to like my brand new book. "Give me a sign! Give me a sign!" I would rail.

Around 9:30 one morning, I turned onto Woodruff, a large seven-lane street, to find not one vehicle on the road, coming or going, which was highly unusual. And spooky, as the fog was very dense, and much lower than usually experienced. Portions of it was swirling about which I had never witnessed beforehand. I was mesmerized by the soundless atmosphere, as it appeared that I was the only person left in the whole wide world. Very weird.

So, as I'm staring at the low-hanging fog, I was shocked to see the nose of a blimp piercing through the fog bank. I couldn't believe my eyes, as it slowly materialized, and seemed to be heading down at an angle, straight towards me! I figured that the pilot didn't realize the fog was so low, and was looking for some landmarks. As I white- knuckled the steering wheel, scenes of police and hospitals instantly filled my mind, even as I recognized that neither the pilot nor I would survive the crash.

Seemingly, at the last minute, the blimp jerked up and slowly moved across the street in front of me, barely skimming across the rooftops, as it headed for the nearby airport. In large letters, painted on the side of the blimp, it said: GOOD YEAR. I happily decided that this was a big thumbs-up from the Universe, which meant that my books were going to do well that year, and I would live to write another day.

I have a wooden sign that always makes me laugh. It says:

IF YOU'RE WAITING FOR A SIGN

THIS IS IT!

NATURE

*Nature in her ever-changing forms
constantly provides signs.*
—Denise Linn

Most people realize that simply being around nature is soothing, cleansing, and balancing. "Allow nature's peace to flow into you as sunshine flows into trees," suggested the great John Muir—the naturalist, author, environmental philosopher, and strong advocate for wilderness preservation. "We feel better after being out in nature," Andrews maintains. Adding, "Nature is probably our greatest healing resource."

As David Spangler explains: " . . . a forest is an ecological unit, in itself, made up of not only trees, but of many other animals and plants, as well." No single species are at risk. Each species is actually an indicator, whose well-being is indicative of the well-being of the forest, as a whole. He cautions, "It is the ecosystem that is at risk, not just a single species." Any dying species disrupts the whole forest (a warning, akin to that of canaries in the coal mines). Unfortunately, nowadays, we would do well to consider the fact that not just one species is at risk, but trees, animals, fish, birds, and bees are dying off, due to pollution of one kind or another.

"Native traditions hold that everything in nature is alive and interacts with us. Nature communicates with us by showing us omens and signs," explains Sandra Ingerman and Llyn Roberts, in their *Speaking with Nature* book. Today, physics uses the term "unified field" to say the same thing. Trish and Rob MacGregor tell us, in *The Synchronicity Highway*, that when we are at one with nature, when we are at one with our environment, when we are " . . . in such a state of being, we intuitively grasp the importance of the signs and symbols that surround us—even if we don't immediately understand their meanings." As such, people are still looking to nature for spiritual guidance, direction, signs, omens, communication, inspiration, and healing.

"Nature and the Earth are conscious; they speak to us now through our dreams, intuition, and deep longings, along with auspicious happenstance," Ingerman and Roberts continue. Note that everything you encounter in nature—all the flora and fauna—has the possibility of being a powerful symbol. Andrews agrees, saying that in order to understand the language of Nature, we must develop the mindset that *everything* has importance and significance. "If it gets our attention, it has meaning." There are two kinds of animal, mineral, and plant encounters: ordinary and extraordinary: An ordinary response is simply a reminder of the wonders of nature. An extraordinary encounter is an unusual experience—the "Wow!" factor, which teaches us something.

Develop a deeper awareness of meaningful nature encounters. "The important experience of synchronicity with non-human nature is often overlooked as being a distinctive experience that can be powerful for the person involved," writes Dr. Matthew J. Zyistra, in his online article for his web site, eye4earth.org. I am in complete agreement. Stay alert to the signs and wonders of nature. Reaffirm and reconnect with nature on a daily basis.

"In every culture human beings have received signs from observing the movements of the natural environment around them. From the way animals migrate, to the location of a lightning strike, to the shapes in the clouds, nature in her ever-changing forms constantly provides signs," Linn maintains. Andrews agrees, saying, ". . . the natural world is one of our most powerful sources of spirit, wonder, and wisdom."

"All symbols portraying Nature are sacred," states Colton. "The first symbols disclosed to the pure in heart are the animal symbols. The next symbols to open are the symbols of plants, trees, seeds, grains. The third symbols to be revealed are the symbol of mountains, water, rivers, oceans, air, earth, fire." Zyistra sums up by saying:

Synchronicity can connect the activities of human beings with apparently unrelated meterologic and geologic events, when meaning occurs. Stay open to nature.

Pay attention to rainbows and snowflakes,
butterflies and the songs of birds,
the crash of storm-driven waves
and the mirror-surface of a quiet pond.
Let the depths of nature
become a part of your innermost being.
—Jonathan Lockwood Hule

Our first national park (actually the world's first national park) was Yellowstone, which was established in 1872. The U.S. National Park Service—which cares for America's special places—celebrated **100** years of stewardship on August 25, 2016. It manages all federal parks, national monuments, historic buildings, and homes preservation sites. It engages citizens, and worldwide visitors, via federal lands and water recreation, nature programs, conservation, and historic properties. There are currently 405 U.S. National park units. Not all states have national parks or memorials, whereas some of the larger states have more than one. Alaska and California have the most. Other units are slated to open in the future. An astounding three million people visit America's national parks annually. Check out the following list of National Parks in your state:

U.S. STATE NATIONAL PARKS

*There is nothing so American
as our National Parks.*
—President Franklin D. Roosevelt

Alabama (0)

Alaska (8) = Denaili National Park and Preserve, Gates of the Artic, Glacier Bay, Katmal, Kenai Fjords, Kobuk Valley, Lake Clark, Wrangell-St. Elias

Arizona (3) = Grand Canyon, Petrified Forest, Saguaro

Arkansas = (1) Hot Springs

California (10) = Channel Islands, Death Valley, Devil's Postpile National Monument, Joshua Tree, Kings Canyon, Lassen Volcanic, Pinnacles, Point Reyes National Seashore, Redwood National and State parks, Sequoia, King Range Conservation Native traditions Park, Yosemite

Colorado (4) = Black Canyon of the Gunnison, Great Sand Dunes, Mesa Verde, Rocky Mountain Connecticut (0)

Delaware (1) = First State National Historic Park District of Columbia (0)

Florida (3) = Biscayne, Dry Tortugas, Everglades

Georgia (0)

Hawaii (2) = Haleakala, Hawaii Volcanoes

Idaho (1) = Yellowstone
Illinois (0)
Indiana (0)
Iowa (0)

Kansas (0)
Kentucky (2) = Mammoth Cave, Abraham Lincoln
    Birthplace Nationall Historic Park

Louisiana (0)

Maine (1) Acadia
Maryland (0)
Massachusetts (1) & Rhode Island (1) = Blackstone
    River Valley National
Heritage Corridor
Michigan (1) = Isle Royale
Minnesota (1) = Voyageurs
Mississippi (0)
Missouri (0)
Montana (2) = Glacier, Yellowstone

Nebraska (0)
Nevada (2) = Great Basin, Tule Springs Fossil Beds
New Hampshire (0)
New Jersey (0)
New Mexico (2) = Carlsbad Caverns, Valles Caldera
    National Preserve
New York (0)

North Carolina (1) = Great Smoky Mountains
North Dakota (1) = Theodore Roosevelt
Ohio (1) = Cuyahoga Valley
Oklahoma (0)
Oregon (1) = Crater Lake

Pennsylvania (0)

South Carolina (1) = Congaree
South Dakota (2) = Badlands, Wind Cave

Tennessee (1) = Great Smokey Mountains
Texas (2) = Big Bend, Guadalupe Mountains

Utah (5) = Arches, Bryce Canyon, Capitol Reef,
    Canyonlands, Zion

Vermont (0)

Washington (3) = Mount Rainier, North Cascades,
    Olympic
West Virginia (0)
Wisconsin =((0)
Wyoming (2) = Grand Teton, Yellowstone
American Samoa (1) = American Samoa
Guam (0)
Northern Marianas (0)
Puerto Rico (0)
U.S. Virgin Islands (1) = Virgin Islands

"In all things of nature there is something of the marvelous," Aristotle said, so many centuries ago. However, you don't have to move to a rural area, a sparsely populated territory, or an inhospitable region, to engage with nature. If you are unable to visit local nature parks or arboretums, or visit state or national parks, you can always watch TV nature programs. Or you can check out nature subjects on your computer for specific content. As both Ingerman and Roberts maintain, "The power and intelligence of the Earth is all around and within us, always accessible."

> *There is no limit to the*
> *symbolism found in nature.*
> —Avia Venefi

ENVIRONMENTS

Different worlds—
different landscapes—
reflect different states of being.
—Ted Andrews

All environments have their own unique qualities. Landscapes, seascapes, cityscapes, and dreamscapes—alongside their elements—not only serve as signs and messages, but they can also serve as catalysts for change. Study and reflection on the important elements of the various settings in which you find yourself—or in your dreamscapes—may shed light upon your issues, energies, lessons, and subtle influences on your future.

"Our natural environment is the symbolic 'jackpot' that holds deeper meaning about who we are and where we are headed on our life path," Venefic says. Feng Shui is the study of how the environment affects those who live in it. Ecology is the study of living things *interacting* within their environment. As Sylvia Earle shows: "Look at the bark of a redwood, and you see moss. If you peer beneath the bits and pieces of moss, you'll see toads, small insects, a whole host of life that prospers in that miniature environment. A lumberman will look at a forest and see so many board feet of lumber. I see a living city." We look at the same environments with different eyes.

TERRARIUM HABITAT

A habitat is the natural or physical home or environment of an animal, plant, or other organism. I was observing a student teacher in the first grade. She was presenting a lesson on ecosystems, and had brought in a 26-gallon terrarium, filled with plants, worms, crickets, and a frog (named Fred). The students listened attentively to the lesson and made their own Food Chain charts. As they finished with their follow-up activities, the children went to observe the terrarium inhabitants. They wanted to get a closer look at Fred, so the student teacher picked him up, and held him, as the pupils oohed and ahhed. Then, with a stricken look on her face, she suddenly yelled, "He peed on me! Fred peed on me!" Oh the shock and horror of it all! Of course, the kids followed along like a Greek chorus, "Fred peed on her! Fred peed on her!" Mass pandemonium, as she charged to the sink, to wash her hands. She got her first understanding, that what she says and does will be mimicked by her students.

As I am writing this, today is Earth Day, 2016. It is an event that is celebrated worldwide, on April 22, to demonstrate support for environmental protection. All of which brings to mind the very first Earth Day, in 1970:

FIRST EARTH DAY

My third graders became heavily absorbed in conservation (land, water, air, animals), ecology, and pollution matters, long before the general public became involved in such. One project mushroomed into another, becoming an all-consuming-year-long interest. A *few* examples of their projects are listed below. (Granted, these activities are pretty old-hat now. But, at the time, it was all new and exciting):

While studying about Water Conservation, the class learned about Archimedes' Principle (water displacement). As a result, the pupils organized a BRICK BRIGADE. They sold bricks for ten cents each, to place in local neighborhood toilet tanks, in an effort to conserve water.

During our LETTER WRITING CAMPAIGN, the students wrote to dozens upon dozens of people and organizations, telling them what we thought of their conservation efforts, both pro and con. Return letters and presents (huge dictionaries, encyclopedias, etc.), arrived on a weekly basis. One company flew a man in from Chicago, just to talk with the class, and take our pictures for their company newsletter. It was quite exciting to check our mailbox each day.

The class collected aluminum cans and newspapers, as part of an ANTI-LITTER CAMPAIGN. With the considerable amount the pupils collected, they voted what they should do with the money.

The students voted to buy three trees, and donate them to our local park, as part of our BEAUTIFCATION CAMPAIGN. The park services made a big deal about the class' decision, and held a special "Planting Day" for us. We walked to the park, and sat on the grass, while the directors in the Parks and Recreation

Department gave speeches about what a "great group" we were (talk about ego-building!). Then each student got to throw a shovelful of dirt into the holes where the trees were located, and a few even got to throw in the giant vitamins. Newspaper reporters, cameramen, parents, and neighbors, watched and applauded the ceremony. (Years later, those former students would return to give me progress reports on "our" trees.)

The class made up their own CONSERVATION SONG and SLOGANS, which they happily sang and chanted, at all of our rallies, demonstrations, and various activities. They also made picket signs and ecology flags, to use at these functions. After all, as we learned, they were teaching others.

Daily, the children would report on articles, conservation, ecology, and related subjects—that they found in newspapers and magazines, which we placed in a giant green CONSERVATION SCRAPBOOK. Towards the end of the school year this 12" x 18", five inch thick, construction paper scrapbook was sent to our state senators, with an accompanying letter, pleading our cause. The senator—with our scrapbook—was on national television, discussing various environmental concerns. He then took it on to Washington, D.C., to show it to everyone in the senate. Talk about positive feedback and reinforcement!!

Meanwhile, I had been asked by our district Science Consultant, to pilot the new SCIS (Science Curriculum Improvement Study) program for that year. It was a fantastic unit, in which *everything* was learned through observation, at unscheduled times.

I chose the POPULATIONS unit, in which the children built six terraria and established plant populations (grass and clover). Crickets were then introduced to the terraria, and the students observed their effect on the plants.

Concurrently, pairs of pupils planted pea seeds in cups, and placed aphids onto the seedlings. As the growth of the aphid populations were observed, the children began to understand the importance of reproduction in population survival and increase.

We also started a fruit fly population (in a container with a banana), and the students observed some of the effects that a rapid, unchecked, increase has on the environment of a population.

The predator-prey relationship was observed, by introducing one chameleon into each terraria. We then continued learning about food chains, food webs, and so forth.

We learned more than I ever thought possible. Word had spread throughout the school population about all the "great stuff" we were doing in our third grade class, but I didn't grasp the strength of the grapevine until the night of open house. I stepped out into the hall, to check on our CONSERVATION DISPLAY, and several minutes later, I couldn't even get back in the classroom. It was hysterical! I had never seen so many people in one room in my entire life (the fire marshal would have had a stroke!). And, lined up along the outside wall, people were patiently waiting their turn to enter. It appeared that kids from every grade level had dragged their parents inside, to see what Room 21 was doing. The noise was deafening.

Throughout the school year, the class had been recording the names of those that were on the ANIMAL ENDANGERED LIST. Finally, the list became so long, that the children became quite concerned, and thought that people should be made aware of the problem. So each child chose an animal that s/he wanted to learn more about. Then each made a written report about the animal, and then made a paper tombstone, including the name of the animal and it's picture. We then held a MOCK FUNERAL, to which they invited their parents and neighbors.

To point out the seriousness of the problem. the students wore black armbands, (out of construction paper), as they solemnly walked to the graveyard (the sandbox). One by one, each child placed his or her tombstone in the sand, and gave a short report about the endangered animal. At length, the sandbox was filled. After flowers were placed over the pretend graves, and a moment of silence was held, the children sang their conservation song, and went back to class.

The impact from the "mourners" was immediate and positive. It was clear that the students had fostered empathy for various animal species. Those in attendance had learned so much! From their varied comments, everyone could tell that this had truly been a consciousness-raising experience.

The point to giving you a small overview of the yearlong class environmental activities, is thus: The third graders were excited to find that while they had been learning about our environment, and what people were doing *to* and *for* it, the older Long Beach City College students had been having parallel learning experiences.

Our class was delighted to hear that LBCC had petitioned the Long Beach City Council for permission to hold an "Earth Day" in celebration of their new insights, and in an effort to educate the general public. The class looked forward to the event. However, the City Council *turned down* their request, saying something to the effect that conservation wasn't of interest to anyone, and nobody knew what an Earth Day was, anyway. The third graders were devastated with the news.

After all they had learned and accomplished throughout the year, the class couldn't believe that adults just weren't interested. Their depression turned to outrage, however, and they began to verbalize their frustration. After a very heated discussion— which was a joy to behold—they decided to take on City Hall. (I do not teach civil disobedience. I teach students to be activists; to stand up for their beliefs; to take action—in a *positive* way—about those things that are important to them; to reach out and make a difference.)

After some initial reluctance, we were finally allowed permission to visit City Hall, to prove to the Council that being environmentally aware citizens *was* important, and that people *were* interested in conservation. The class presented their posters, speeches, flags, and chants. Apparently, other adults had also voiced their opinions on the subject. And the Long Beach City Council revoted on the issue, and gave LBCC permission to continue in their plans for an Earth Day celebration.

LBCC was so thankful for our help, that their journalism department wrote an article about our class in their own school newspaper. The whole center two pages were written about our efforts on their behalf. And they extended an invitation to us, to be "special guests" at their Earth Day celebration. All of the children learned a valuable lesson: People—no matter their age—*can* and *do* make a difference.

VOLCANO EXPLOSION

A fourth grade class, cattycornered from the office, finally exploded the volcano they had made, a culmination activity for their earth-science unit, an event that happened yearly in the same month. As expected, the stifling odor of sulphur and smoke mushroomed in the classroom, and billowed down the hall. At first sniff, the class vacated the premises, and retired to Goldenrod Park, several blocks away, where they missed all of the resultant excitement.

Since none of the administrators were on the grounds—who expected this seasonal episode—the entirely *new* office staff immediately dialed 911. And you can guess what happened after that: Assorted fire engines of all shapes and sizes, ambulances, various police cars, helicopters, media vans, parents, neighbors, and so forth, descended upon the school. The full catastrophe. The entire school population of 1200 students stood out on the far playground, for close to an hour, watching the fire marshals try to pinpoint the problem. It was clear from the lingering smell that a fire was somewhere! At length, other fourth grade teachers—finally noticing that one of their grade level classes was missing—figured out the situation, informed the authorities, and everyone finally left the property, and the students went back to their classrooms. Whew!

The following compilation list of environmental terms—and their significant meanings—is provided via Andrews, Colton, Linn, Meinberg, Upczak, and Zyistra. Use this list for dream interpretation, or for understanding the influence of the various places or situations in which you find yourself:

ENVIRONMENTAL MEANINGS

Abyss = danger, impassable chasm, fear, dark, foreboding

Backcountry = sparsely inhabited rural areas
Backwoods = remote, uncleared forest land
Beaches/Dunes = unique challenges, adaptability, extreme life, healing,
spiritual doorways
Boulders = obstacles, barriers, stumbling blocks
Bushland = uncultivated and undeveloped

Cave = subconscious, isolation, retreat, ("to cave in to difficulties"), or renewal, rebirth
City/Suburban = adaptability, variety, flexibility, community and social issues
Cliff/Edges/Overhang = potential hazard, a critical time, a chancy situation, a momentous decision, taking a risk ("a leap of faith"), or a big change, infinite possibilities, activity, dynamic, alive, cliff-hanger

Desert = hardiness, spiritual rejuvenation, purification, and emotional clarity, or harsh trials, loneliness, isolation, desolation, or turn your desert into a garden

Dunes = extreme life, harsh conditions, adaptability, challenges, or need for healing, balance, and reflection

Earth = receptive, rejuvenating, earthy, foundation, grounded

Earthquake: a sudden, violent shaking of the ground, sometimes causing great destruction; a great upheaval; quakes make us reevaluate our lives in a deep way; they are catalysts; abrupt change, great change, new growth, new experiences ("a whole lot of shaking going on"), flexible, adaptable

Edges = the busiest environmental zones for growth and change, borders and boundaries that support wildlife and plants that depend on several types of environments for survival

Floods = overwhelming emotions

Forests/Woodlands = abundance, growth, strength, protection, safety, refuge, the unconscious mind ("The creation of a thousand forests is in one acorn."—Ralph Waldo Emerson)

Fountain = crystal clear, intuition, free-flowing emotions, youth, spiritual wellspring

Garden = beauty, peace, creativity, nurture, weeding out, harvesting, movement, growth

Geyser = a great release, emotional pressure or energy

Glacier = frozen emotions

Heat/Hot = passion, intensity ("in heat"), anger

Hinterland = uncharted areas

Hot Springs = healing, purification

Island = isolating yourself or being self-contained ("no man is an island")

Jungle = wild, overgrown, dense, tangled, nearly impenetrable, unruly, less civilized ("it's a jungle out there")

Lakes/Ponds = oasis, nourishment of body, mind, and spirit

Land = firm ground, solid foundation, supportive structures, connection to Earth

Lava = release your suppressed anger

Marshes/Wetlands/Swamps/Bogs = bogged down, decomposition, new growth, transition, emotions

Meadows/Fields = beauty, harmony, balance, sanctuary, nurturing, rest, abundance, nourishment, fertility

Mountain = obstacle or opportunity, attainable or insurmountable, progression, uplifting, overcoming attitude or ("making a mountain out of a molehill"), or spiritual attainment, powerful

Mud = stuck, unclear, childlike joy

Oasis = a refuge, a personal retreat, rejuvenation

Ocean/Seas = subconscious mind, intuitive power, primordial wisdom possibilities, birth or smooth sailing

Orchard = bearing the fruits of your labor, a fruitful life

Paradise = innocence, beauty, peace, love

Pond = emotions, intuition

Potholes = stepping blindly into danger

Prairies/Plains = abundance, possibilities, new homes, new winds, changes

Quicksand = pulled under, fear, struggle

Rivers/Streams = creation, shape-shifting, time, evolution, yielding, pliant, adjusting, shifting and flowing

Rock/Stone = strong, permanence, solidity, grounding

Rural = countryside, rustic, desolate, hard

Sand = no permanence (the shifting sands of circumstance), irritations, small annoyances, changes, or all is illusion

Sky = reach for the sky, the sky isn't falling or identify with the sky, rather than the passing clouds that obscure it

Smoke = warning, danger ("where there's smoke, there's fire"), a lack of clarity

Star = star quality, shine brightly, leadership

Swamp = bogged down, no clarity, overwhelmed

Tidal Waves = complete chaos, huge emotional upheaval

Tide = ebb and flow of emotions, movement to and fro, up and down, inward and outward, change, or abundant and lean, doors opening and closing

Underground = subconscious mind

Valley = protection, safety, beneficial, fertility, creativity, home, refuge, opportunities, or low point of life, all experiences are valuable

Vineyard = harvesting the fruits of your experience

Volcano = explosion of suppressed emotions and passions; healing

Water = source of all life, fertility, emotions, feelings, vitality, clarity, intuitions, psychic perceptions, subconscious mind

Waterfall = emotional release, recharging, healing

Wave = surging forward, great emotional strength and power

Wetlands = transitions

*The voyage of discovery
is not in seeking new landscapes
but in having new eyes.*
—Marcel Proust

WEATHER

Wherever you go,
no matter the weather,
always bring your own sunshine.
—Anthony J. D'Agelo

The word meterologic relates to the branch of science concerned with the processes and phenomena of the atmosphere, including the weather and climate. Signs and symbols can be found within any kind of weather, serving as a catalyst for a variety of insights and changes. "If your life is a journey, then emotions are the natural weather fronts you pass through," explains Millman.

A POWERFUL WISH

When in the fifth grade, on a family vacation across the states, we were driving in the middle of nowhere, through a seemingly endless Arizona desert. Although the weather was clear, the car radio mentioned a chance of flash floods, and I excitedly said that I would *love* to see one, since I couldn't picture it in my mind. My mother became quite upset that I would say such a thing, and admonished me for doing so, ending with, *"Be careful what you wish for!"*

The sentence was barely out of her mouth, when, on cue, a powerful flash flood swept across the highway, washing the pickup truck in front of us off the road, landing it, nose-down in a ditch. An enormous amount of water coursed around it, with such force that the doors couldn't be opened.

All traffic was stopped in both directions, unable to cross the dangerous fast-moving water, and we had a front-row seat to the mighty destruction that a flash flood can wreak. I was further shocked to see that the driver of the pickup was a young woman—gender issues were stuck in 1949—and that she had a small baby with her. Both were crying, so we didn't know if they were injured, or just freaking out about the unexpected situation. But we were unable to help.

Since cellphones were nonexistent at that time, someone had to turn around, and drive all the way back to the closest town, to get the sheriff. He and a helper finally arrived, with a heavier truck, ropes, and chains. We watched the ropes being used, as the sheriff battled through the water to rescue the baby first, and then went back to pull the woman to safety. Both were hauled out through the cab back window. It was a long and arduous process. At length, with chains, the heavier truck pulled the pickup back onto the highway, and shortly thereafter, the flash flood had finally lost its punch. At that point, traffic was able to continue on, as if nothing had happened. Mother acted as if the whole experience was my fault, and I realized just how *powerful* our spoken words are.

"Spoken words are the foundation of what we continually create in our own lives. We should never underestimate or limit their tremendous power," Halberstam and Leventhal tell us, in their first book, *Small Miracles*.

FUNERAL

It was a dark and dismal day, for our small family memorial at the grave site. The rain had stopped, just as my brother began the eulogy for our father, as I was too undone to even say anything. After the prayers were offered, we were just lingering there for a minute or two, when the sun suddenly burst through a hole in the dark clouds, and sent a brilliant shaft of light, in a straight line slanted across the sky, ending directly upon Dad's coffin. It was a pretty amazing sight! The display didn't last long, however, as the clouds quickly covered the hole. Now to any other onlookers observing that bright ray of light, it would have no personal meaning, other than, "How beautiful!" or "How unusual!" But to me, it represented a great validation, which put my mind at rest.

With this truly synchronistic moment, I breathed a sigh of relief, knowing that Dad had successfully crossed to the other side, and that he had met those spirit relatives who loved him, and everything was now as it should be: he was safe and secure. I had worried about Dad, and his disbelief in an afterlife, and felt that his attitude might delay the transformation process in some way.

As a youngster, he had come to question the fundamentalist beliefs of the religion in which he was raised. Later, as a university student, with the mind of a scientist (physics), he raised even more questions. Upon graduation, he had received straight A's in all his classes, except for one B in a required comparative religion course. The professor had explained that "Nobody is perfect!" and refused to give A grades to anyone. Ever. That seemed to be the straw that broke the camel's back for Dad, and he became a dyed-in-the-wool agnostic. In his latter years, however, it became apparent that he was considering a greater plan, even though we weren't privy to his conclusions.

Note that the same incident, occurring to several people, will often yield completely different experiences, one synchronistic and meaningful, and the others, not.

RAIN, RAIN, GO AWAY

Whatever the weather, there is always something new to learn. When I was a brand new teacher, it had rained for a solid week, with no end in sight. The streets were not only flooded, but the water lapped over the front door steps.

It was dark, and the storm was fierce, when I saw three of my third grade boys slogging through water up to their knees, struggling in the torrent to get to school. I stopped my car, and they hopped inside, as the water crested the running board. They thanked me profusely for the ride. I slowly maneuvered down the street—that was akin to a flowing river—and we finally got to school in one piece. After the fact, I was told, in no uncertain terms, to *never* do that again, due to insurance problems. Who knew? I just thought I was helping.

Rainbows apologize for angry skies.
—Sylvia Voirol

Like the weather, and the seasons, your emotions are always changing. "Stormy weather can reflect an inner storm. Rain can connote grief or emotional purification. Fog can indicate feeling that you can't see your life clearly," explains Linn. The following compilation list of meterologic conditions—and their significant meanings—are offered via Andrews, Colton, Linn, Meinberg, and Upczak. Use this list for dream interpretations, or for understanding the emotions involved with the weather in which you are experiencing:

WEATHER MEANINGS

Aurora = light, glowing, colors, complexity, moving, beautiful

Autumn = completion

Balmy =warm, gentle, calm, tranquil or foolish, eccentric

Blizzard = immense emotional upheaval, deceived ("snow job")

Bluster/Blustery = strong, wild, violent & abrupt outbursts, loud, aggressive, rant, rave, bullying, sound off, by doesn't always follow through

Breeze/Breezy = pleasant, relaxed, informal, cheerily, fresh

Cloud = mystery, illusions, intuition, dreams, secrets, emotions, revelation, or drifting

Cloud Burst = suddenly violent, heavy

Cold = unemotional, unfriendly, unwelcoming ("cold and calculating"), no longer fresh ("cold case")

Comet = tremendous personal and spiritual expansion

Condensation = moisture, steam, evaporation (crying?)

Contrail = a white streak across the sky (Are you leaving your mark? Are you making a fast getaway?)

Cyclone = a tropical storm, windstorm, whirlwind, tempest, gale

Dawn = wake-up call, a fresh start, a new beginning, a new awakening, seeing the light, illumination.

Disturbance = upset, annoyance, irritation, intrusion, disruption, distraction, interference trouble, hassle

Downpour = heavy deluge of problems or emotions

Drizzle = light, spray, mist, sprinkle, spotty

Drought = lack, shortage, serious damage

Dry = dehydrated, parched, withered, shriveled, wilted

Dust devil = strong, well-formed, long-lived whirlwind, swirls dust, debris, and sand to great heights

Dust Storm = strong, turbulent wind carrying clouds of dust, soil, and sand over a large area

Earthquake = abrupt change, great change, new growth, new experiences, ("a whole lot of shaking going on"), flexible, adaptable

Fire = power, potency, energy, sexual passion ("burning with desire"), anger ("fiery words")

Flash Flood = a sudden and destructive local flood, due to heavy rain

Flood = complete emotional chaos, overwhelmed, release old beliefs, growth, regeneration

Fog/Mist = emotional or mental confusion, obstacle, unconscious mind, magic, mystery, confusion, secrets

Freeze/Frozen = fortresslike inner privacy, closing yourself off, isolation, blocked emotions, trapped energy, paranoia, solitary activities

Frigid = cold, frozen emotions, bitter, stiff and formal

Frost = frozen, covered with ice crystals, an icy, unbending nature

Funnel Cloud = the core of a tornado or waterspout

Gale = a very strong wind, outburst

Glacial = ice cold, freezing, sub-zero, unfriendly, hostile, unwelcoming

Gust = a brief, strong rush of wind, blow, bluster, roar

Gully Washer = short, heavy rainstorm

Haboob = intense, vast, duststorm

Hail = pellots of frozen ice

Haze = blur, confusion, daze, muddle

Heat/Hot = high temperature, anger, intensity, passion

Heat Wave = a prolonged of heat or anger

Hurricane = a tropical storm with a violent wind, in a circular fashion

Ice = frozen emotions, precarious circumstance, slipping, unsure

Ice Storm = a storm of freezing rain or emotions

Icicles = releasing blocked emotions; better flow

Lightning = great power and breakthrough ahead, or life is brief

Melting = freeing repressed emotions
Mist = a cloud of tiny water droplets
Monsoon = a seasonal wind and rain (Asia)
Moon = romance, fertility, inner reflection, inspiration
Mud = stuck, unclear, childlike joy
Muggy = sticky, oppressive, unpleasantly warm and humid

Outlook = view, vista, panorama, scene
Overcast = dull, chilly, cloudy, gray

Precipitation = drizzle, rain, sleet, snow, hail
Pressure = force, coerce, press, persuasion, influence, demand, intimidate

Rain = emotions, crying, cleansing, renewal, growth, healing, emotional rebirth, gifts from the heavens, fertility, or destruction ("into each life some rain must fall")
Rainbow = blessings, relationships, celebration, joy, hope, end of difficulties

Sandstorm =a strong, turbulent wind carrying clouds of sand
Season = four divisions of the year, marked by weather patterns (spring, summer, fall, winter)

Shadow = fear, illusion, unknown parts of yourself that you've denied, repressed, devalued, and disowned, accept yourself as you are, nothing left to hide

Shower = a brief, light fall of rain, snow, sleet, or hail

Sleet = ice pellets mixed with rain or snow

Slush = partially melted snow or ice

Smog = fog or haze mixed with smoke

Smoke = warning, danger ("where there's smoke, there's fire")

Snow = cleansing, purity, fresh start, new beginning

Spring = new growth, new possibilities, new life

Sprinkle = a light scatter or trickle of rain

Star = light, guidance, insight

Steam = water converted into vapor ("he was steamed")

Storm = understand the storms in which you find yourself, there are lessons in all of them, internal conflict, we are still standing after the storm

Summer = fulfillment, confidence, happiness, contentment

Sun = power, strength, energy, success, clarity, inner light

Sunny = bright with sunlight ("a sunny disposition")

Sunrise = when the morning sun appears over the eastern horizon

Sunset = in the evening when the sun disappears below the western horizon

Temperature = the degree or intensity of heat

Tempest = a violent, windy storm, gale, with rain, hail, or snow

Thaw = when ice or snow becomes liquid

Tidal Wave = enormous emotional upheaval

Tide = movement, ebb and flow, in and out, abundant and lean, change

Thunder = noise, fear, surprise, staggered, declare it, loud and clear

Thunderstorm = a storm with thunder, lightning, and heavy rain

Tornado = a mobile, rotating, funnel cloud with destructive winds

Turbulence = violent and unsteady movement, conflict, confusion

Twilight = soft, glowing light in the sky as the sun sets, half-light, gloom, semidarkness, or obscurity, ambiguity, gradual decline

Twister = a tornado

Typhoon = a tropical storm (of the Indian or western Pacific oceans)

Unstable = to fall, change, fail, give way, unsteady, wobbly, shaky, or unbalanced ("mentally unstable"), unsound mind ("mentally ill")

Updraft = an upward current of air

Vapor = a substance diffused and suspend in the air (haze, mist, steam, moisture, condensation, talking in a boasting or pompous way

Vapor Trail = contrail

Visibility = to see or be seen

Vortex = a mass of whirling fluid or air, whirlpool, whirlwind

Warm = comfortable temperature;, or confortable expressions, friendly, kind, pleasant, or getting closer ("you're getting warmer")

Warning = possible danger, problems, unpleasant situations

Water = a colorless, transparent, odorless, tasteless liquid that forms the lakes, rivers, oceans, and rain, and is the basic fluid in all living organisms

Waterspout = a rotating column of water, a tornado over water

Wave = a long body of water, curling into an arched form, and breaking on the shore

Whirlwind = a column of rapidly moving air in a cylindrical or funnel shape

Whiteout = a blizzard that reduces visibility to near zero

Wind = thought, intellect, breath, and spirit, subtle, a dramatic shift in consciousness, or blowhard

Weather is a great metaphor for life,
sometimes it's good, sometimes it's bad,
and there's nothing much you can do about it,
but carry an umbrella.
—Terri Guillmets

TREES

Except during the nine months
before he draws his first breath,
no man manages his affaires
as well as a tree does.
—George Bernard Shaw

It is truly understandable as to why trees were worshipped in the long, long ago. To paraphrase Ernest and Joanna Lehner, in their book, *Folklore and Symbolism of Flowers, Plants, and Trees*, trees were not only the largest living and growing things around humans, but they were always there, amongst them as children, youngsters, men and women, and elders. They would learn that the trees were already standing in the same groves, when their parents and grandparents were children themselves. They would grasp the idea that those same trees would still be standing, long after they, themselves would be gone, when their children's children would be no more, and when their great, great, grandchildren would be growing old. As such, trees became symbols of strength, fertility, and eternity.

SAY WHAT?

> In the midst of winter, a friend had a visitor from another country. At a large party, the foreigner asked me—in all seriousness—"Do you belong to that religion that *kills* trees?" I was astounded. Talk about a different perspective during the Christmas season!

Throughout the changes in history, the Tree of Life symbols were included in all the beliefs and religions in the eastern and western world. And the Tree of Knowledge of Good and Evil became the tree of mortals in the biblical Garden of Eden. And, of course, you have your own Family Tree.

Andrews tells us that there is much truth to the idea that hugging a tree is healthy for you. "Each tree has its own unique and powerful energy field." Different trees can be hugged for different results. "Our energy field interacts with that of the tree, resulting in specific effects." He continues, saying that the stronger the tree, "and the longer the contact with it, the greater the energy exchange. It then becomes a catalyst, affecting us and our life on some level."

Besides the general meaning involved for every species, each individual tree has its own properties (ancient or young, straight, leaning, or crooked, just beginning to leaf, in full foliage, losing its leaves, or it has lost all leaves).

GIANT EUCALYPTUS TREE

One February, Southern California was hit by a devastating storm. Thundering mudslides crushed homes, hurricane winds smashed thousands of trees, vehicles were swept away, a dam collapsed, five bridges washed out, animals escaped the zoo, corpses floated out of a cemetery, and an entire mountain community vanished.

Clean up for our city took three weeks. It was estimated that 500 trees were toppled in Long Beach alone. So, after things had dried out for a bit, I took my third graders to the park to survey the damage.

Giant Eucalyptus trees were scattered every which way, like pick up sticks. In order to get the feel of the immense size of these trees, I had the class play follow-the-leader upon the trunk of a fallen tree. With varying degrees of agility, we climbed up through the massive root system, and then walked single-file along the length of the tree. This was scary for some of the children, as they didn't like being so far off the ground (so several scooted across on their bottoms). The pupils began helping each other on and off the tree, as well as giving encouragement and prodding to those who needed it. (It hadn't occurred to me that this experience would be anything more than totally FUN! Wrong. But then, I was a tomboy as a child, and would have *loved* doing this.)

After the students had gained some confidence in their tree-walking, they began to circle faster and faster, from the root system, across the trunk to the tip of the treetop, where they would jump down (assisted by two others standing on the ground), and run around to begin again at the roots. It became a joyous occasion to all. They had conquered their fears, and were happily playing together, which showed just how far their relationships had matured.

The clearest way into the Universe is through a forest wilderness."
—John Muir

There are an estimated 100,000 tree species in the world, which is about 25 percent of all living plant species. The following short compilation of common trees—and their significant meanings—is provided via Andrews, Colton, the Lehners, Linn, and Presley. Use this list for dream interpretation, or for understanding your favorite trees:

TREE MEANINGS

Alder = foundation, protection, trust, open perceptions, prophetic dreams, insight, survival
Almond = sweetness of life, delicacy, fertility, gentle
Apple = hidden knowledge, youthfulness, beauty, joy, strong, gentle, giving, playful, happiness, magic and mystical, healing ("an apple a day keeps the doctor away")
Ash = protection, strength, connection, wisdom
Aspen = calming, fearlessness, determination, new opportunities, exploring, expanding, searching, healing, rebirth, resurrection, or quaking in fear
Avocado = spiritual nourishment

Banana = prosperity, potent fertility, or danger (due to Tarantulas)
Birch = balance, healing, new dimensions, cleansing, new beginnings, opportunities, energy, purpose
Blackthorn = called "The Mother of the Wood," unexpected changes, bad luck, battle, strife, resentment, confusion, refusing to see the truth,

pain, wounding, damage, a thorny experience or self-conquest, transcendence

Cedar = protection, cleansing, strength, healing
Cherry = faith, trust, the juices of life, rebirth, new awakenings, new insights
Coconut = nourishment, challenge, fortitude
Cypress = awakens the comfort of home and mother, facing one's fears, sacrificing for a greater cause

Date Palm = The date Palm is the most ancient symbol of the Tree of Life, because it produced a new branch each month. It is still used today as a religious symbol, by both Christians and Jews. It is a symbol of triumph over adversity. It is still considered as the Tree of Life, because of its fruit— the date—which, either fresh or dried, is the main food supply for people and animals.
Dogwood = joy, beauty, unexpected surprise

Elder = birth and death, beginning and end, transition, protection, magic, healing, opportunities, creativity, change, balance, regeneration
Eucalyptus = balance, protection, healing, clarifies dreams and emotions, slow down, detoxify your life

Fig = peace, abundance, trust your intuition. The fig tree was considered to be the sacred tree of

Buddha. There are hundreds of species of the fig tree, and it is revered nearly everywhere as the Tree of Life and Knowledge.

Fir = honesty, truth, strength, longevity

Hawthorn = Hope, happiness, fertility, change, transformation, death (In England, the hawthorn is known as the mayflower tree, in honor of the month in which it blooms. The Pilgrims named their famous ship, The Mayflower.)

Hazel = called the Tree of Knowledge, learning, wisdom, strength, playfulness, exhilaration, enchantment, divination, inspiration, poetry

Heather = forward looking to new colors, new endeavors, fertility, solid foundations, creative endeavors, unfolding inner potentials, immortality

Holly = spiritual warrior, protection, healing, align energies, focus, goals

Jacaranda = beauty, good luck, magic, rebirth, spring, or "purple panic" denoting student stress: (In Australia, if a student has not begun seriously studying for final exams by the time the jacaranda trees bloom, all is lost.) Beautiful, purple Jacaranda trees form a magnificent canopy over many streets in my neighborhood. They blossom twice a year, causing picturesque purple tunnels to drive through. When the slightest breeze occurs, a dazzling "purple rain" follows. It is a spectacular sight. Despite their beauty, the trees are notoriously messy. Purple flowers litter the streets, sidewalks, front yards, and cars. It is a lovely sight to those who do not have to deal with the untidiness of it all. Neighbors love to witness the Jacarandas in bloom, while, at the same time, they are so thankful that the trees are on someone else's property, so they aren't tracking purple onto their rugs and carpets, or into their cars.)

Lemon = freshness, cleansing, clearing emotions, clarity of thought, sensitive to color, stimulates friendship and love, healing

Lilac = mental clarity, protection, productivity, awakens the kundalini, activates clairvoyance, harmony, healing, balance, spiritualizes the intellect

Lime = intimacy, attraction, lovers

Magnolia = intuition, idealism, love, healing, long-lasting fidelity, be true to your heart

Maple = balance, intuition, creativity, expression, aspirations

Oak = strength, endurance, confidence, reflection, fertility, immortality (In pre-historic times, the oak was the most sacred, because it was considered to be the first created tree, and that humanity sprang from it.)

Olive = peace, harmony, trust, sensitivity, inner guidance, health and wellness, regeneration, clairaudience, hope

Orange = generosity, hospitality, abundance, clarity of emotions, energy, release fears, longevity

Palm = the Tree of Peace, calming, protective energy, warmth, freedom, celebrate

Pine = balances strong emotions and feelings of guilt, protection, kind, sensitive, clear perspective, heightens psychic sensitivity, creative energies, spiritual clarity, purification

Redwood = ancient protection, balance, new perspectives, spiritual vision, changes, time, longevity

Spruce = understanding, trust intuition, calming, amplifies healing, focus, stimulates dreams, guidance

Walnut = powerful transitions, mystical, hidden wisdom, universal knowledge,

Willow = flexible, beautiful, alleviates headaches and body pains, or sadness, grieving ("weeping willow)

THE OFFICIAL U.S. NATIONAL TREE

The American national tree is the oak, which is considered to be the grandest tree on earth— the largest, the oldest, and the most magnificent. Joseph Bitner Wirthlin explained, "Giant oak trees . . . have deep root systems that can extend two-and-one-half times their height. Such trees are rarely blown down regardless of how violent the storms may be." So oaks also have great staying power.

I love trees! As such, I recently bought a breathtaking photograph of one of the oldest and most storied trees in North America, the 1,500-year-old *Angel Oak*, by Will Conner. I ordered the large size (21"x 45"), and had it professionally framed, and hung. Visitors can't believe it is a photograph, since it looks like a gorgeous fantasy painting. It is a wonderful addition to my art collection.

> *Today's mighty oak*
> *is just yesterday's nut,*
> *that held its ground.*
> —David Icke

OFFICIAL U.S. STATE TREES

All of the fifty states, and several U.S. territories have designated an official tree. All of the state trees, with the exception of Hawaii, are native to the state in which they are designated.

Alabama = longleaf pine
Alaska = Sitka spruce
Arizona = palo verde
Arkansas = pine

California = coast redwood
Colorado = blue spruce
Connecticut = white oak

Delaware = American holly
District of Columbia = scarlet oak

Florida = cabbage palmetto

Georgia = live oak

Hawaii = candlenut tree (kukui)

Idaho = western white pine
Illinois = white oak
Indiana = tulip poplar
Iowa = oak

Kansas = eastern cottonwood

Kentucky = tulip poplar

Louisiana = bald cypress

Maine = eastern white pine
Maryland = white oak
Massachusetts = American elm
Michigan = eastern white pine
Minnesota = red pine
Mississippi = magnolia
Missouri = flowering dogwood
Montana = ponderosa pine

Nebraska = eastern cottonwood
Nevada = singleleaf pinyon pine
New Hampshire = paper birch
New Jersey = northern red oak
New Mexico = pinyon pine
New York = sugar maple
North Carolina = longleaf pine
North Dakota = American elm

Ohio = Ohio buckeye
Oklahoma = eastern redbud
Oregon = Douglas fir

Pennsylvania = eastern hemlock

Rhode Island = red maple

South Carolina = cabbage palmetto

South Dakota = Black Hills spruce

Tennessee = tulip poplar
Texas = pecan
Utah = blue spruce

Vermont = sugar maple

Washington = western hemlock
West Virginia = sugar maple
Wisconsin = sugar maple
Wyoming = plains cottonwood

Guam = ifil or ifit
Northern Marianas = flame
Puerto Rico = silk-cotton
U.S. Virgin Islands = none

The wonder is that
we can see these trees
and not wonder more.
—Ralph Waldo Emerson

FLOWERS

Flowers are a happy sign
of beauty and unfoldment.
—Denise Linn

Flowers are a wonderful substitute for words. Flowers speak to us in many ways, through their form, color, beauty, and fragrance. Any and all flowers can be living reminders to: Have patience in the seed that is about to sprout; we all bloom in different ways; we all flower in different fields; we come from the same soil; we all need light, nurturing and caring; we sprout, blossom, and grow together; as well as, take the time to smell the flowers, or, allow yourself to be seen. ("Flowers don't open and close according to who is walking by. They open and show their beauty regardless," says Rebecca Campbell).

Flowers are inspiring, and raise the energy of any occasion. They are a fundamental part of most rites of passage: weddings, births, baptisms, dedications, birthdays, graduations, religious ceremonies, funerals, and celebrations of all kinds. They bring beauty, energy, fragrance, and uplifting vibrations to any event. In addition, flowers are used in meditation, and as food, medicine, and in various art forms. They bring joy to the recipients, as well as the senders.

Each unplanned flower has a message for you, as do those flowers that are sent to you. "Flowers are often the messengers of our emotions, hopes, and dreams. Through them we send and receive," Halberstam and Leventhal tell us, in *Small Miracles II*. In the bygone days of chivalry, flirtation, and courtesy, flowers and poems were the only gifts exchanged by lovers. So Flower Language was most important in the 18th and 19th centuries.

The Lehners tell us that: "Every bouquet and garland, nosegay and posy, corsage and boutonniere, festoon and wreath, was carefully composed according to its legendary meaning." A difference was shown between a single flower, a handful, or a bouquet. A bouquet means sincere gratitude, while a single rose amplifies the meaning of the color (a single red rose means "I REALLY love you").

Color plays an important part of the flower message. Although each species has its own unique vibration, individual flowers have different meanings. As *The Farmer's Almanac* website explains, the same flowers with specific coloring have different meanings attached to each. For instance, a pink rose means perfect happiness, a red rose says, "I love you", a white rose signifies innocence and purity, whereas a yellow rose denotes a decrease in love, or even jealousy. Similarly, a pink carnation means affection, a red carnation means "I love you", a white carnation means pure love, a striped carnation shows regret that love isn't shared, and a yellow carnation implies disappointment or rejection.

DELIVERY

> Intermittently, when my husband was feeling especially loving, or as a way to say, "I'm sorry," he would send gorgeous flower displays to my school. They were absolutely fantastic, which everyone felt impelled to comment on. The office would call me, to come pick them up. They always looked so beautiful on my desk. Unfortunately, one of my new pupils was allergic to flowers. So whenever they were delivered, thereafter, the flowers had to stay in the office. Everyone loved them, but eventually he stopped sending them, since I got to enjoy them less than others.

All flowers are symbolic of beauty, youth, vitality, happiness, and joy. As Ralph Waldo Emerson said, "The earth laughs in flowers." Note that the meaning you give to each flower, may be far afield from the general association. (If truth be told, many of the meanings on various lists, don't match each other.) If the flower is beautiful, that should be enough for us.

The total number of described flower species exceeds 230,000, while many tropical species are as yet unnamed. As such, a much smaller number of flower species—that may be recognized by you— is offered below. The following short compilation list of flowers, both wild and domestic—and their significant meanings—is offered via books by Andrews, Colton, the Lehners, and various websites, such as The Farmer's Almanac, whats-your-sign. com, Gift Tree, and 50states.com. Use this list for dream interpretation, or for understanding the flower that has unexpectedly appeared in your life

FLOWER MEANINGS

Aster = powerful love

Baby's Breath = delicate, sweet, beauty, gentleness, modest, moving= gently forward
Black-Eyed Susan = change, intuitive faculties, insight, overcoming resistance, justice
Buttercup = self-worth, success in every environment, healing, understanding, opportunities, expressive, words affect all things

Carnation = fascination, deep love, new opportunities, healing. The pink carnation symbolizes mother-love. As such, it was chosen as the emblem for the Mother's Day holiday (the second Sunday in May) in the U.S., to honor motherhood.

Chrysanthemum = cheerfulness, wonderful friend, healing, vitality, long life, keep your heart open, a messenger (a red chrysanthemum says: "I love you")

Cornflower = new life, energy, clairvoyance, psychic energies, creative forces, balance

Cosmos = order, peace, serenity

Daffodil = spring, new beginnings, renewal, potential, new life, inner beauty, clarity, inspiration, creativity

Daisy = freshness, innocence, loyalty, purity, creativity, hope, unequaled love ("He loves me, he loves me not" divination technique)

Dandelion = happiness, faithfulness, look beyond the surface

Forget-me-not = true love, memories, relationships, connections, new perspectives, and the symbol of remembrance

Gardenia = you're lovely, secret love, emotional protection, telepathy

Geranium = true friendship, infatuation, new happiness and vitality, new opportunities, or stupidity, folly

Gladiola = high aspirations, remembering, calm, integrity, spiritual impulses, or give me a break, I'm really sincere

Goldenrod = fulfillment, resolution, healing powers, be true to yourself, trust in your dreams, follow your own path, encouragement

Hawthorn = hope, only the best, supreme happiness

Heather = admiration, solitude

Hibiscus = rebirth, youthfulness, sexual energies, fame, riches

Holly = hope, domestic happiness or defense

Honeysuckle = strong and everlasting love

Hyacinth = love, fertility, gentleness, creative, constancy of love, fertility, games and sports, or rashness, overcome grief and depression and jealousy

Hydrangea = thank you for understanding, frigidity, heartlessness

Iris = a message, your friendship means so much to me, hope, peace, new birth, faith, wisdom, valor, power

Ivy = friendship, continuity

Jasmine = sweet love, prophetic dreams, a messenger, good spirits, discriminating, changes, major transformation

Jonquil = affection, sympathy

Lavender = calm, soothing

Lilac = joy of youth

Lily = virginity, purity, majesty, transformation

Lily of the Valley = sweetness, humility, new birth, purity, humility, you've made my life complete, mother's love and energies, return to happiness

Lotus = spiritual, higher knowledge, new vision, the soul rising from the confusion of matter into the clarity of enlightenment

Magnolia = nobility

Marigold = undying love, content, words have healing power, trust intuition, psychic sensitivities, sacrifice, or cruelty, grief, jealousy

Mistletoe = kiss me, affection, to surmount difficulties

Morning Glory = affection, peaceful dreams, break old habits, be spontaneous, sensitivity

Narcissus = "stay just the way you are"

Oleander = caution

Orange Blossom = innocence, loveliness, chastity, purity, eternal love, marriage, fruitfulness

Orchid = love, beauty, refinement, strong sexual energies, balance energies

Pansy = thoughts, think before acting, consider all possibilities

Peony = shame, happy marriage, happy life, healing, artistic abilities

Petunia = proper behavior, enthusiasm, or resentment, anger

Poppy = pleasure, wealth, success, imagination, new creative energies, don't hold back, or eternal sleep, oblivion

Primrose = I can't live without you

Rose = love, desire. romance, happiness, healing, new birth, considered to be the "queen of flowers"

Seeds = germination, new beginnings, sprout ("as you sow, so shall you reap")

Snapdragon = protection, guidance, strength, clairaudience

Snowdrop = hope, beauty (This flower used to be considered bad luck, because it seemed to always grown in graveyards.)

Spider flower = weave something new, avoid entanglements of the past, versatility, suppleness, transformation, learning, elope with me

Sunflower = self-actualization, happiness, healing, well-being, protection. great joy

Sweetpea = goodbye, departure, blissful pleasure, thank you

Tiger Lily = balance, strength, success

Tulip = declaration of love, perfect lover, trust, stand out, dream awareness, clairaudience, clarity, discernment, discrimination, greater vision, success. (The tulip is the national emblem of Holland.)

Violet = loyalty, devotion, faithfulness, modesty, simplicity, lucky opportunities, psychic sensitivity, dreams, well-being

Water Lily = creative, manifestation, psychic sensitivity, new opportunities, money, wealth

Zinnia = humor, courage, reawaken inner child, encouragement, hope. thoughts of absent friends

> *Coincidences are not exotic flowers*
> *growing under special circumstances.*
> *They are more like*
> *common wildflowers*
> *popping up all around us.*
> —Bernard D. Beitman, M.D.

OFFICIAL U.S. NATIONAL FLOWER

Did you know that the official national flower of the United States is the rose (as is four states)? It is a symbol of love and beauty, as well as war and politics. Since the rose has been around for 35 million years, it also represents staying power.

OFFICIAL U.S. STATE FLOWERS

Each of the states, and five inhabited U.S. territories have an official flower. There are more than 15,000 wildflowers found in the U.S. Half of the states have a wildflower as their official flower. Oddly, many of the state flowers are from other parts of the world, and are not native to the state, but were chosen for their beauty or importance.

Alabama = camellia
Alaska = forget me not Arizona saguaro cactus
   blossom
Arkansas = apple blossom

California = California poppy
Colorado = Rocky Mountain columbine
Connecticut = mountain laural

Delaware = peach blossom
District of Columbia = American Beauty rose
Florida = orange blossom

Georgia = Cherokee rose

Hawaii = pua aloalo

Idaho = syringa mock orange
Illinois = purple violet
Indiana = peony
Iowa = wild prairie rose

Kansas = sunflower
Kentucky = goldenrod

Louisiana = magnolia

Maine = eastern white pine tassel and cone
Maryland = black-eyed susan
Massachusetts = mayflower
Michigan = apple blossom
Minnesota = pink and white lady slipper
Mississippi = magnolia
Missouri = hawthorn
Montana = bitterroot

Nebraska = goldenrod
Nevada = bristlecone pine
New Hampshire = purple lilac
New Jersey = violet
New Mexico = yucca
New York = rose
North Carolina = longleaf pine
North Dakota = wild prairie rose

Ohio = scarlet carnation
Oklahoma = mistletoe
Oregon = Oregon grape

Pennsylvania = mountain laurel

Rhode Island = violet

South Carolina = yellow Jessamine
South Dakota = pasque flower

Tennessee = iris
Texas = Texas bluebonnet

Utah = sego lily

Vermont = red clover
Virginia = flowering dogwood

Washington = coast rhododendron
West Virginia = rhododendron
Wisconsin = violet
Wyoming = Indian paintbrush

American Samoa = red ginger
Guam = ifil or ifit
Northern Marianas = plumeria
Puerto Rico = Puerto Rico hibiscus
U.S. Virgin Islands = yellow trumpetbush

MONTHLY FLOWER LISTS

Throughout my life, I have seen monthly lists of flowers in calendars, diaries, and magazine articles, but never paid much attention to them, other than the fact that there was only one flower mentioned per month. (As a child or teen, no one ever gave be flowers for my birthday!) However, I just came across a list by *The Old Farmers' Almanac* (1792-2016), which listed *two* flowers per month, and thought it may be of interest to you, for various birthday or anniversary dates:

January
Carnation & Snowdrop

July
Larkspur & Waterlily

February
Violet & Primrose

August
Gladiolus & Poppy

March
Jonquil & Daffodil

September
Aster & Morning Glory

April
Sweet Pea & Daisy

October
Marigold & Cosmos

May
Lily of the Valley
& Hawthorn

November
Chrysanthemum

December
Narcissus & Holly

June
Rose & Honeysuckle

It is not an accident when a flower
"mistakenly" appears in your garden.
—Denise Linn

ROCKS, STONES, & GEMS

Crystals, minerals, and stones—
these sparkling treasures from deep within the earth,
can help distract you from any troubling thoughts
that might be getting in the way of your progress.
—Margaret Ann Lembo

I consider rocks and stones to be the first history books. Wisdom is inside them. Stones have always attracted me, because the artist in me loves their beauty. I love their colors, size, shape, weight, and patterns. As such, stones, crystals, minerals, and geodes are sitting in every single room in my house. Some are so big, or so heavy, they can't be easily moved. The smallest ones are placed together in bowls, to encourage touching, holding, and rubbing. Stones are a way for me to keep in touch with the earth and nature.

Stories, "sayings, and proverbs, based on rocks," the geologist, Andrew Alden, tells us, "refer to both the symbolic qualities of stones, their permanence and resistance; their weight, inertness and contrast to living things; their imperviousness, obstruction and infertility; their strength, passivity and solidity; their anonymity, single-mindedness and monotony."

Although most people use the words rock and stone interchangeably—as do several dictionaries—there *is* a clear difference. Both David B. Williams, in his GeologyWriter.com website, and Nedha writing for the DifferenceBetween.com website, explain: Rock is large, heavy, and immovable, especially raw material in situ (like the Rocky Mountains, or the Rock of Gibraltar). It is hard, symbolizing strength and endurance (" . . . in matters of principle, stand like a rock."—Thomas Jefferson). Stone is a smaller or moderate-sized piece of rock, easily moveable, and is usually smoother, connoting human handling or human use.

Rock = solid ("like a rock," "bedrock," "rock steady," "rock-hearted," "rock solid"), large, heavy, immoveable, permanence, grounded, stability, foundation, strength, endurance, cold, silent
Stone = a smaller piece of rock ("stepping stone"), cold ("stone cold"), wealth, power ("stonewalled"), healing

Stones, gemstones, and crystals, have been used as talismans, totems, and amulets, since before recorded history. From river rocks to huge boulders (like Stonehenge), and stones of every kind and size, all have been called "the bones of Mother Earth." As such, they are an integral part of our history. Throughout the centuries, various cultures have contributed to their legends and lore, ascribing qualities that are both genuine and superstitious.

A jewel is a gemstone that is turned into a work of art, whether by the cut, finish, or polish of the gem, or the setting it goes into. A jewel is a sign of that which is precious and brilliant, which signals the coming of riches and true happiness. To paraphrase Pearl and Ponzlov: Like a diamond or a jewel, what we do constantly in this life is polish facets of ourselves, allowing the best parts of ourselves to surface. And with the polishing, comes understanding and growth.

> *Each gem has its own energy*
> *and its own symbolism.*
> —Denise Linn

Each stone has its own energy and symbolism. The following short list of gems—and their significant meanings—is a compilation from several books via Colton, Lembo, and various websites like *The Old Farmer's Almanac*, whats-your-sign. com, Beadage, Gemstone Dictionary, OutofStress, GemSelect, and Emily Gems. Note that some books or websites, emphasize emotional meanings, some emphasize health issues, while others emphasize spiritual descriptions. Each gemstone listed below has a short and sweet version of its overall meaning. Use this list for dream interpretation, or for understanding the stone or gem that has unexpectedly appeared in your life:

GEMSTONE MEANINGS

Agate = protection from bad dreams, stress, and energy draining

Amber = grounding, boundaries, stability, protection, powerful ancient wisdom, understanding, helps memory, positive change, detoxification, transforms emotions

Amethyst = stress reliever, peace, focuses thoughts and actions, humility, promotes selflessness, reverence, restful sleep, clear dreams and recollection

Aquamarine = calming, soothing, cleansing, relaxing, light-heartedness, inspiring, truth, trust, good luck, fearlessness, protection, safe journey over the seas, considered to be the treasure of mermaids

Blue Topaz – encourages higher thinking, associated with courage, overcoming fears and obstacles, inspiration, creativity, mental clarity

Carnelian = grounding, curiosity, initiative, boosts confidence and motivation, heals past emotional stress, used to stimulate appetite, eases cramps, and lessens back pain.

Citrine = promotes optimism and mental focus, positive thoughts, attracts abundance, awakens awareness

Crystal = clarity, spiritual energy

Diamond = most valued, clarity, hope, balance, wisdom, innocence, constancy, bonds relationships. enhances love, abundance, courage, sparkle ("you are a diamond with many facets and flaws"), the higher self, spiritual initiation

Emerald = healing emotions, power, infusion of love, aides fertility, magic, and business connections, predicts the future, psychic powers, lifts depression, relieves insomnia, enhances memory and mental clarity

Garnet = awakening, passionate devotion, increases vitality and stamina, attracts good luck in business, determination, creative powers inspires enlightenment

Jade = harmony, good luck, wisdom, intuition, beneficial to the heart and lungs, prosperity, growth, abundance, bountiful harvests, positive thinking, good outcomes, spiritual development

Lapis Lazuli = a strong protection stone, grounding, boosts immune system and blood circulation, reduces pain and inflammation, lowers anxiety, harmony, remember dreams, improves concentration and focus, calming, inner peace

Onyx = repels negativity, enhances determination and perseverance, grounding, mental focus, peaceful sleep, releases fear, protection

Opal = protection, love, passion, promotes imagination, dreams, healing

Pearl = beauty, perfections, rare, value, purity, dignity, charity, honesty, wisdom, integrity, transmutation, spiritual guidance

Peridot = prosperity, growth, alleviates depression, anger, fear, anxiety, transformation, inner strength, unlimited possibilities

Quartz = love, energy, balances, cleanses, and heals physical, mental, stays focused, emotional conditions, clarity, memory recall, spiritual attunement

Ruby= healing, love, passion, self-knowledge, selflessness, protector from misfortune, inner strength, spiritual and mystical experiences

Sapphire = law, non-judging, centering, higher mind, reduces inflammation, fevers, and nose bleeds, aids in communication, intuition, and relaxation, peace, happiness, meditation tool, truth, wisdom

Smoky Quartz = endurance, serenity, calmness, positive thoughts

Tiger's Eye = mental and emotional benefits, transforms stress and anxiety into productive energy, aides digestion, relieves high blood pressure, balance, strength

Topaz = heals, energizes, balances, calms, strength, promotes truth and forgiveness, increase awareness, loyalty, faithfulness, friendship, purifies emotions, true love, success, joy

Turquoise = attracts money, success, love, friendship, timing, balances mood swings, calming, divine inspiration

Various states in the U.S. have significant mineral deposits, enough to promote an interest in their natural resources, history, and tourism. As such, they have officially created a state mineral, rock, stone, or gemstone. Not every state has shown such an interest, however.

OFFICIAL U.S. STATE MINERALS, STONES, & GEMS

Alabama = Hermatite, Marble, Star blue quartz
Alaska = Gold, no stone, Nephrite jade
Arizona = Copper, no stone, Turquoise
Arkansas = Quartz, Bauxite, Diamond

California = Gold, Serpentine, Benitoite
Colorado = Rhodochrosite, Yule marble, Acquamarine
Connecticut = Almandite Garnet

Delaware = Sillimanite, no stone, no gem
District of Columbia = none

Florida = no mineral, Agatized Coral, Moonstone

Georgia = Staurolite, no stone, quartz

Hawaii = no mineral, no stone, black coral

Idaho = no mineral, no stone, Star garnet
Illinois = Fluoite, no stone, no gem
Indiana = no mineral, Salem limestone, no gem
Iowa = no mineral, quartz Geode, no gem

Kansas = none
Kentucky = Coal. Kentucky Agate, Freshwater pearl

Louisiana = Agate, no stone, Lapearlite (Eastern oyster shell)

Maine = no mineral, no stone, Tourmaline
Maryland = no mineral, no stone, Patuxent River Stone agate
Massachusetts = Babingtonite, Roxbury Puddingstone, Rhodonite
Michigan = no mineral, Petoskey stone fossilized coral, Chlorastrolite
Minnesota = no mineral, no stone, Lake Superior agate
Mississippi = no mineral, Petrified wood, no gem
Missouri =Galena, Mozarkite, no gem
Montana = no mineral, no stone, Montana Sapphire and Montana Agate

Nebraska = no mineral, Prairie agate, Blue agate
Nevada = Silver, Sandstone, Black fire opal and Turquoise
New Hampshire = Beryl, Granite, Smokey quartz
New Jersey = none
New Mexico = no mineral, no stone, Turquoise
New York = no mineral, no stone, Garnet
North Carolina = Gold, Granite, Emerald
North Dakota = none

Ohio = no mineral, no stone, Ohio flint

Oklahoma = no mineral, Rose Rock, no gem
Oregon = no mineral, Thunderegg agate, Oregon
    sunstone labradorite

Pennsylvania = none

Rhode Island = Bowenite serpentine, Cumberlandite,
    no gem
South Carolina = no mineral, Blue granite, Amethyst
South Dakota = no mineral, no stone, Fairburn agate

Tennessee = Agate, Limestone, Tennessee River Pearl
Texas = Silver, Oligocene petrified palmwood,
    Texas blue topaz

Utah = Copper, Coal, Topaz

Vermont = Talc, Granite and Marble and Slate,
    Grossular garnet
Virginia = none

Washington = no mineral, no stone, Petrified wood
West Virginia = no mineral, Bituminous Cot,
    Mississippian fossil coral
Wisconsin = Galena, Red granite, no gem
Wyoming = no mineral, no stone, Wyoming
    nephrite jade

Check out Wikipedia's free encyclopedia's List of
U.S. State Minerals, Rocks, Stones, and Gemstones,
which has amazing color photographs of each item.

MONTHLY BIRTHSTONE LIST

The wearing of birthstones was thought to ensure good health and good luck.

January	**July**
Garnet	Ruby
February	**August**
Amethyst	Peridot
March	**September**
Aquamarine	Sapphire
April	**October**
Diamond	Opal
May	**November**
Emerald	Topaz
June	**December**
Pearl	Turquoise

I adore wearing gems,
but not because they are mine.
You can't possess radiance,
you can only admire it.
—Elizabeth Taylor

ANNIVERSARY STONES

The following list is provided by Antoinette Matlins, P.G., in her latest *Colored Gemstones* (3rd Edition) guide:

1. Gold	13. Citrine
2. Garnet	14. Opal
3. Pearl	15. Ruby
4. Blue Topaz	20. Emerald
5. Sapphire	25. Silver jubilee
6. Amethyst	30. Pearl jubilee
7. Onyx	35. Emerald
8. Tourmaline	40. Ruby
9. Lapis lazuli	45. Sapphire
10. Diamond	50. Golden jubilee
11. Turquoise	55. Alexandrite
12. Jade	60. Diamond jubilee

An anniversary is the perfect time
to celebrate all the missed opportunities
to correct a mistake
and even take vows to renew it.
—Bauvard

SYMBOLS

Far more powerful than religion,
far more powerful than money,
or even land, or violence,
are symbols.
Symbols are stories.
Symbols are pictures,
or items, or ideas
that represent something else.
These symbols are
everywhere around you.

—Lia Habel

SYMBOLS

It all depends on how we look at things,
and not how they are in themselves.
—Carl Jung

Symbols are everywhere. Every day, we are surrounded by symbols, so much so, that we rarely think about them: a smiley face, a skull and crossbones, a peace sign, biohazard, gender symbols, and such. Each has a thought or message it wants to convey. Symbols are easy to understand, regardless of language, culture, or ethnic background. Yet, Day maintains, ". . . symbols are a highly sophisticated form of communication. They convey a great deal of detail much more economically than do literal words."

CADUCEUS

My husband has had several heart operations over the years, as well as long-term diabetes. As such, he is prone to losing his balance, at times. He has fallen down steps, and twice, when on his daily walk through the park, he fell. As such, he had a large caduceus tattooed on his inner arm, that states that he is diabetic. It runs a good eight inches long on his forearm. So if anyone were to find him lying in the park, or the victim of an accident, they would know to call the paramedics, forthwith. He has more confidence, and feels safer now.

Each and every one of us have had unusual encounters that can be interpreted symbolically in various ways. Be alert and alive to recurring themes, and remain open to the symbols in your life. "Synchronicity manifests itself in clusters of numbers, names, objects, words, and symbols," say Trish and Rob MacGregor, in *The Seven Secrets of Synchronicity.* "In every moment of your life you are walking in a "forest of symbols" that are constantly reflecting your personal reality," Linn tells us. "Stay open and available to all the forms of meaning," advises Moss. Understand that " . . . incidents in waking life speak to us exactly like dream symbols."

To paraphrase Ted Andrews, in his equally popular *Animal-Wise* book, discussing animal encounters: Suppose one evening, you drive home through a cloud of skunk spray; when home, you turn on the TV, to find a science program on skunks; you flip the channel to a Pepe LaPew cartoon; you walk through a store to find stuffed skunk toys hanging about, and so forth. You realize that you are in the midst of a symbolic cluster, and need to consider the meaning involved. Is there something going on in your life that smells to high heaven? Are you a doormat? Do you need to hold your ground? You may need to look at boundary issues. Are you being intruded upon? Or might there be wrong timing involved somewhere? Or could you be taking a bath in a financial matter? Note that the skunk is nonviolent, but highly effective. Skunks are symbolically recognized for protection, independence, and self-respect.

"Symbols are the language of the soul," stated Colton. And *anything* can act as a symbol. A symbol is a person or a thing that stands for something else, especially a material object that represents something abstract, such as flags, seals, coats of arms, emblems, statues, an image, or a gesture.

A flag is a piece of rectangular fabric, with a distinctive design, used as a symbol for countries, states, organizations, or as a signaling device. A pennant is a longer piece of fabric that tapers to a point, that signifies something of special significance. It is a kind of accolade, award, or honor, showing approval or distinction. Pennants are often flown from the masthead of a vessel, or are an emblem of victory (sports, or some sort of championship), or they signify special places (universities, cities, vacation spots, national parks).

MANZANAR

Since the early 50s, as a youngster, my husband Wayne, and his family, had driven up Highway 395 to the High Sierras, every year, for the Opening Day of trout season. Over those years, they went from campfires to condos, as their financial situation improved. Each time they passed Manzanar, his mother would always explain how that was the place in which local Japanese were *unjustly* incarcerated during WWII. It was one of ten camps, across the nation, in which over 10,000 citizens were forced to relocate. It is considered to be the best-preserved of the former campsites, and is now called the Manzanar National Historic Site.

Later in the 80s, while working at Rancho Los Amigos Hospital, Wayne met a Japanese- American, that volunteered for a study with a new artificial leg. He had lost his leg in Italy in WWII, while fighting with the 442 (the all Japanese-American unit). They often talked about fishing, and the drive north on Highway 395. He told Wayne that he had been at Manzanar, and had volunteered for the 442nd Infantry Regimental Combat

Team, and was shipped out of state for training, and later to Italy.

As a war buff, Wayne learned so much about his experiences, and it was a really big deal for him to hear about the most decorated unit in U.S. military history. It was awarded eight Presidential Unit Citations, and 21 of its members were awarded the Medal of Honor.

On his last visit to the hospital, for the follow-up on his artificial leg, he gave Wayne a large felt pennant, that read: CAMP SHELBY—HOME OF THE 442. Wow! Wayne felt so honored, and expressed his thanks. He kept it for years, until he heard that Manzanar was looking for items to place in their brand new museum. So he took the pennant with him, on one of his yearly trout trips with his brother, and stopped at Manzanar. He donated the pennant to one of the curators, who was very excited about it. So it had a new home. It had come full circle.

Citizens in English-speaking countries, as well as most European countries, know that a red octagon sign symbolizes STOP, even without the word, and a red cross stands for the International

Red Cross organization, while a red rose symbolizes love. Some symbols are from your country, your culture, your society, or your religion. As such, for hundreds of years, people have focused on those ancestral symbols, which are now held in the collective conscious. Although most symbols are seen visually, they can also appear via smell (the odor of roses, smoke, perfume), sound, or touch. Then, too, you have your own personal symbols.

For instance, "Flags are potent images expressing the identity and distilling the character of the particular peoples they signify into a single, powerful image," explains Joseph. Whereas a hand salute is a gesture of respect, honor, recognition, greeting, praise, or disrespect, via individuals, groups, and subgroups, from various countries. Gestures are culture-specific, conveying very different meanings in different social or cultural settings.

Emanuel Swedenborg (1688-1772), a scientist, philosopher, and theologian, viewed the universe as "symbolic in every detail," and that all aspects of nature are reflections, emblems, and symbols of corresponding characteristics of man. Thus, Craig S. Bell writes in his *Comprehending Coincidence*, " . . . a certain mood, emotion, or human quality corresponds with and is symbolized by a particular musical note, a specific color, a type of tree, a certain animal, a particular mineral or element, a flower or plant, a planet or constellation—and so on, all symbolic of each other and all representations of underlying qualities that are found in humans."

"The first symbols disclosed . . . are the animal symbols. The next symbols to open are the symbols of plants, trees, seeds, and grain. The third symbols to be revealed are the symbols of mountains, water, rivers, oceans, air, earth, fire," and so forth, explains Colton.

Swami Vivekananada Bengali (1863-1902), an Indian Hindu monk, who first brought Hinduism and Yoga to America, would agree. "In one sense, we cannot think but in symbols; words themselves are symbols of thought. In another sense, everything in the universe may be looked upon as a symbol . . ." Symbols are viewed as such by intellectuals, philosophers, scientists, metaphysicians, and artists the world over. Bell adds, " . . . the role of symbols in our lives may be far more extensive than we normally are aware of."

"Synchronicities cluster around significant events," explains Richo. And clusters of symbols, be they words, phrases, numbers, animals, or whatever, are sure to grab our attention. They tend to jolt us out of our everyday uniformity. Clusters, in whatever form, tend to relay the message that something unusual is taking place, and that we need to pay attention.

Any experience can become a wake-up call that expands awareness. To paraphrase Joseph, synchronicities speak to you in symbols meant specifically for you. Since there is no exact definition for any symbol, all symbols are open to interpretation. The more you pay attention to symbols, the more everything in your life makes sense.

All symbols have
multiple meanings.
—Robert H. Hopcke. MFT

ANIMALS

See a world where all animals—
large and small, courageous and timid,
wild and domesticated, strong and weak—
are treated as we ourselves
want to be treated.
—The Intenders of the Highest Good

I would posit that each and every one of us has had some kind of unique experience with either a domestic or wild animal. Good or bad, painful or marvelous, such encounters stand firmly in our memory banks. Understand that "Messengers do not always assume human shape. Validation may come in many forms," Halberstam and Leventhal tell us, in *Small Miracles II*. "Animals in symbols and dreams, allegories, parables, and meditative experience, correlate to the emotion and thoughts of man, identifying his character and temperament," explains Colton. She goes on to say, "The behavior and temperament of an animal, bird, or reptile, seen in dream or mediation, describes certain inclinations or tendencies of a person."

"Any creature may be a messenger, a vehicle for synchronicity," say the MacGregors. "When an animal appears to you—especially one you wouldn't normally see in the course of your ordinary day, or that shows up under unusual circumstances— consider what you were thinking about, or doing at the time." They add that the sighting could be a verification that you're making the right decision or warning you that you're about to make the wrong decision. Look for clues to its message: "What do its habitat, physical characteristics, behavior and habits tell you? What are its most recognized qualities?" They further say that you may need to see how the animal is portrayed in folklore, mythology, and fairy tales, before you completely understand what the synchronicity means.

Animals offer a powerful link to our inner selves. Pay attention when an animal suddenly appears in your life. Every animal is a messenger, if we just watch and listen. We must practice keen awareness. Richo agrees: "Animals, both when we are awake and in our dreams, serve as guides." They appear unexpectedly, in unusual places. They escort you along your path. Animals are considered to be teachers, shamans, and messengers.

All animals have certain skills to teach, and certain knowledge to share, if we look at them as messengers. As Andrews tells us, in his book *Animal-Wise*, "Everyone has been touched by animals in some way, either in life or in dreams, and always the difficulty is determining what it means."

For instance: I have an irrational fear of big dogs. I don't know why, or how this fear first came about. I can't remember there ever having been a time when something wild and wooly could have happened to me with a dog, or even having observed such. At any rate, I am uncomfortable around big dogs, in the extreme, and have very little to do with any dogs, at all. I generally avoid them. I never show my fear, especially around children, as I don't want to be a negative role model for them.

BIG DOGS

Feeling under the weather the night before, and still not feeling quite up to par in the morning, I called in sick at work. By early afternoon, however, I was feeling much better. Sitting in the front of the house, staring out the large window, I was bored out of my mind. Nothing was happening, since all the neighbors were at work or school. All was quiet on the block. I was wishing that I was at school, with all the students, where something exciting would be going on.

Suddenly, a ratty old car shot down the street, with two teenagers in it. My first thought was, *"Why aren't they in school?"* The girl was driving, and stopped the car in front of the driveway, catycornered across from my house. The boy got out and walked up the driveway, so I figured they were looking to score some drugs, and would be sorely disappointed, because no one was home. I expected to see him return forthwith.

Not so. I heard the back door slam with such force, that the windows shook. The phone was at my elbow, so I immediately called 911, and told the operator that I was witnessing a burglary in process. She advised me to stay on the line, and describe everything I was seeing. So I did.

The girl had made the turn in the cul-de-sac, and came back to idle in front of the driveway. Soon, the guy came out, laden down with two large speakers, a skateboard, and a bunch of other stuff. When the girl saw all the stolen property, she was trying to decide what to do—as the car made several fast start/stop/start/stop/start/stop movements, and then she took off in a cloud of smoke, leaving the guy with a shocked look on his face. He immediately dropped the skateboard, on the ground, and took off on it. The speakers became too unwieldy, so he dropped them on other front lawns, as he zoomed by. I lost track of him as he rounded the corner onto Stearnlee Street.

A few minutes later, five police cars zoomed onto the block, so I went out to talk with the officers. I told them that they just missed the teenager, and they said don't worry about it, as he was being taken care of. The officer in charge asked me if I had ever been in the house. And I said, of course. So he asked if I would escort him through the rooms, to see if any other damage had occurred. So, the two of us went in the backdoor, and I was talking a mile a minute, as I trailed him through the kitchen, and started into the hall, where we abruptly froze, as we were met by a huge, low-growling Doberman Pinscher. Uh-oh.

The three of us didn't move, and the only sound was coming from the dog. As the officer gradually got his gun out, he quietly whispered that we were going to slooowly back out, because otherwise, there would be blood and guts all over the place. Yowsers! As I began moving backwards, two other

Doberman Pinschers came around from the living room, and stood behind me. Not good. Although they were big, they seemed to be young, and didn't know quite what to do. So we both, in slow-motion, finally backed out of the door.

As we walked down the driveway, on rubbery legs, thanking our lucky stars that we were in one piece, we saw that more squad cars had arrived on the scene. An undercover officer was also there, who, it turned out was the father of the girl in question. After she had left her partner in crime, she called her dad, to tell him that she was in big trouble.

In addition, a huge school bus full of students, was also parked on our street. When I asked why it was there, I was told that the skateboarder had tossed a number of items, in his attempt to get away, and had accidently thrown an item through one of the open windows of the bus. So the bus became a part of the crime scene.

There were so many vehicles parked on our little cul-de-sac street, that the neighbors couldn't get through to their own houses, when they came home from work. So the block went from absolutely nothing going on, to a full-out catastrophe. And I certainly got my wish: something exciting going on, with students involved. Oh, boy.

YET ANOTHER DOG

I was minding my own business, walking down the Stearnlee sidewalk, on the way to my friend's house, when I saw a huge dog heading toward me. Uh-oh. Although it was on a leash, it was towing its handler along at a fast clip. The young woman was ineffectively trying her best to stop the dog as it powered on, and was having no luck in doing so. The dog was much heavier than she was, and running fast, so the best she could do was yell and flap her free arm, as the dog dragged her on. It was totally out-of-control, and suddenly focused on me, as it loudly barked, and lunged forward. The poor woman had a stricken look on her face, recognizing a disaster in the making. I knew I was a goner. It was clear this wasn't going to end well, as I had nothing in my hands with which to fight off an attack. It was a foregone conclusion. We weren't but about twelve feet apart—and I was bracing for the onslaught—when, at the perfect time, two little dogs in a yard across the street, started barking, and yipping, and yapping, and generally making a fuss, acting all macho, while safely behind a chain link fence. The charging dog suddenly changed course, and shot cattycornered across the street, in an effort to tear them limb from limb—while the woman vainly tried to stop him. They were all loudly snarling, growling, snapping, barking and shouting at each other, as I turned left at the corner, and went on to my friend's house. A minute off, here or there, and I would have been toast. But I had lived to face another day.

So the above stories are simply to show that I am queasy around big dogs. I try to stay away from them, but they somehow keep finding me. I'm determined to get over my fear before I leave this world, and I figure that I have 24 years left, to do so (I'm shooting for 100). Anyway, they are a lead-in to the following story:

COYOTE

I have always been afraid of big dogs (although I don't know why). One dark, early morning, I was walking down the middle of Stearnlee street (in an effort not to wake the neighborhood dogs, that would start barking and howling and awaken their owners), on my way to the local park. When I was just about eight feet from the park curb, I saw a coyote loping along, from my left. I stopped dead still. The coyote walked right in front of me, as if it didn't even recognize me as a human, and halted. I seemed to be just a stationary object that it was hiding behind. I bizarrely thought that, if I were to slightly bend over, I could actually pet it. Then I questioned *why* I would want to pet such a big wild animal, when I was afraid of tame dogs that were smaller. We both stood silently for a short while, without moving a muscle. Then the coyote quickly inclined its head back in the direction from which I came, and suddenly took off like a shot from a cannon. I was immediately concerned for the small dogs, cats, and rabbits in the surrounding neighborhood. Then I wondered about where the coyote's den was, and if cubs were involved, and where would they find enough to eat, and so forth. And I was dumbfounded at my initial reaction, realizing that I knew next to nothing about coyotes.

I only had the cartoon Wile E. Coyote as a model, and knew that coyotes are considered to be tricksters in folklore. That was the sum total of my knowledge about them. So I nixed the idea of my walk through the park, as I hot-footed it home to safety, and my computer, to research coyotes.

Know that each of us experience unusual situations that we interpret symbolically in different ways. I'm still trying to figure out the message involved in the above coyote event, other than the observation that I can laugh at myself for being afraid *after* the occurrence. Long after the fact, the following memory came to me:

COYOTE KIDS

Later, in the dim mists of my long-ago memory, I realized that when I was six or seven years old, we neighborhood children banded together in our own Coyote Kids Club. In order to be a member, each individual had to vow, that even if it was pouring rain outside, and he or she heard our coyote distress call, that each would immediately come outside to help one another—*even if their mothers or fathers wouldn't let them.* Yikes! We pictured ourselves climbing out of our bedroom windows, if we couldn't sneak out the door. Oh, the horror of it all! After much consideration, everyone solemnly promised. It was a very big deal. And we swore that it was a *secret*, and that we would *never* tell anyone, as we were united as a family of coyotes. If someone didn't show up in the rain, that kid would be banished from the club. Forever. Oh, the horror of it all! Luckily, it never rained, so no one was ever put to the test. I don't think we did much more than run around barking, yipping, howling, and growling, while hiding from imaginary unwanted predators, and pouncing on our own prey. I imagine the adults on the block were tired of our noisy antics, and were pleased when we eventually turned to quieter distractions. Come to think of it, maybe this was why I have such a soft place in my heart for coyotes. They get such terrible press in the news media these days. (Oops! I just realized that I broke my long-ago vow.)

Every animal has its own symbol, which varies between countries and cultures and ages. Know that some dyed-in-the-wool meanings won't connect with you or your situation, in the slightest.

SILKY

Early morning, before school began, I passed by the playground, on my way back from the office to my classroom. The pupil's voices had changed from a low roar to the high-pitched squeal of delighted children running wild. Uh-oh. Something's afoot. I 180ed the grounds like a cop looking for telltale signs of a crime in progress; the youngsters could be playing just a simple game of hide and seek, or a more serious one of hit and run, or the dreaded search and destroy.

Hordes of students—of all ages—were running and screaming in mock terror, while a little blond, second grader chased them all around the playground. *What in the world . . .?!* I thought, as I stood transfixed, watching the noisy demonstration. I couldn't figure out why the little girl was holding her hand in front of her in such an awkward position, as she merrily charged after everyone.

"Dead rats! Dead rats!" the pupils obligingly shouted out to me—on cue—as they gaily galloped by, happily

pointing and gesturing behind them. They thundered past in vast circles. Then I spied a long thin tail hanging out of her hand. Uh-oh. Why do I always notice these things? I complained to myself, as I motioned the little girl over.

"What do you have in your hand?" I asked, as a curious crowd of onlookers quickly gathered around.

"Just Silky," she said, as she proudly showed me a small *live* mouse.

"Whatever made you bring Silky here?" I further questioned her.

"My class is going on a field trip to the zoo today," she explained, "and I wanted to show Silky the animals." Ah, I decided, an act of love, not willful disobedience.

After I explained the field trip rules ("Sorry, no pets allowed!"), I sent her with a messenger to a kindergarten room that houses a vast supply of animals, to see if they could provide Silky with a safe habitat for the day. Problem solved. Timing is everything!

THE PETTING FARM

Often, the things children learn or experience on a field trip, are not what was expected, or intended, or preferred, given options:

The first unusual event at the petting farm took place when the pigs snuffled around the first and second graders' feet, causing them to make loud and teary objections. Then the goats decided, en masse, to eat the students' name tags off their clothes. Although this was found to be hilarious by some, many children found it to be a very intimidating experience, and they needed to be calmed and soothed about the situation. (Not only were they being pushed around by pigs and goats, but they were now bereft of their identities.)

Of course, without name tags, none of the helpers knew which schools the children belonged to, so everyone just sort of grabbed small groups of pupils to herd around the farm. Some of the braver children picked up the hens and carried them wherever they went.

One of the tour guides was telling facts about the various farm animals. She pointed out the donkey, informing the third graders that the animal was ten years old and pregnant. One young girl shouted in a shocked voice, "If I was ten years old and pregnant, my mom would *kill* me!"

Later, as the students were dutifully lined up behind a row of cows, the milker launched into a discussion, and began to demonstrate how to milk them. Many pupils found this disgusting enough ("Tha's nasty!"), when, as if at a given signal, several cows lifted their tails and deficated all over the closest children. Mass pandemonium! ("Dookey!", "Poo-poo!", "Ka-ka!", "*Shit!*"). The noise was deafening, the smell overpowering, and the students were a sartorial mess! Everyone charged off in different directions, trying to get out of the cows' immediate target area. The odor radiated from their bodies in nearly visible wavy lines, like a cartoon rendition of a skunk. Did any fumes ever smell quite so bad? Could we all die from the smell? On the bus ride back to school, I thanked my lucky stars that

my nose didn't work as well as others.
Ee-i-ee-i-o.

Animals can represent " . . . a primal, instinctive part of your being. If the animals are wild and ferocious, they can be a sign of the more primitive, aggressive part of your nature. If the animals are tame, they can represent the controlled expression of your instinctual nature. And if they are wild and free, they can symbolize your connection to nature," Linn explains. Note that a specific kind of insect, sea creature, bird, reptile, or animal, in addition to its sex, or color, and sometimes size, rends a different meaning.

The wiseGeek team website, identified 5,416 mammal species wordwide, which does not account for those species not yet identified. And researchers report 15,000 new species (of all kinds) each year, so the number of mammal species is probably far above that given number.

> *We can judge the heart of a man*
> *by his treatment of animals.*
> —Immanual Kant

The following compilation list of common mammals—and their significant meanings—is offered via Andrews, Arruda, Colton, Hallberg, Linn, Love, the MacGregors, Sander, Upczak, and Venefica. Use the list for dream interpretation, or for understanding the symbolism of the animal that has unexpectedly appeared in your life. Remember that your experience of each animal may mean something entirely different. As the MacGregors point out: "If you're terrified of dogs, for example, you probably won't associate them with unconditional love and acceptance." Like me.

ANIMAL SYMBOLOGY

Anteater = disturber, fear bringer, upsetting routines

Antelope = speed, action, adaptability

Armadillo = retreating personality, trust, peace, pacifism, reclusive, curiosity, protection, guardedness, boundaries, searching, discovering

Ape/Gorilla = primal power, solid, strength, copying or mimicking

Badger = self-reliant, aggressive behavior, bold, willingness to fight

Bat = see through illusions, new beginnings, intuition, dreaming, visions, communication, powerful medicine, happiness, good fortune, rebirth, initiation, journey, high potential, or death, superstition, fear of the unknown, witchcraft

Bear = strength, courage, tenacity, powerful, protection, sleep, awakening the unconscious, introspection, renewal, resurrection, confidence, authority, nurturing, or loner

Beaver = busy, industrious, taking action, builder, creating, serious, accomplishment, building your dreams

Bobcat = secrets, silence

Buffalo = power, sustenance, abundance, harvest, plenty

Bull = strength, fighting ability, force, power, male fertility

Buzzard/Vulture = picked on, preyed upon, clean up messy situations

Camel = endurance, perseverance, successful, change of place

Caribou = travel, migration, movement

Cat = freedom, liberty, independence, flexibility, persistence, relaxation, looking for another opportunity, change in sleeping habits, luxury, grace, or mystery, magic, psychic, spiritual power

Cheetah = speed

Chimpanzee = innovation

Chipmunk = play, work, storage,

Cow = peace, patience, endurance, nourishment

Coyote = wisdom, humor, laughter, or folly, stealthy, cowardly, scavenger, outcast, trickster

Deer = gentleness, gracefulness, innocence, love, compassion, camouflage

Dog = friend, companion, guardian, protection, loyalty, faithful, unconditional love, acceptance, intelligence, vitality

Donkey = humility, patience, or stubborn, unyielding, burden carrier

Elephant = power, gentleness, memory, dignity, intelligence, thick-skinned, strength, obstacle remover, peace, ancient power, royalty (Trunk up symbolizes success and victory, whereas trunk down means inverted, malicious, insensitive, force without passion, defeat

Elk = power, strength, steadfast, surefooted, beauty, stamina, dignity

Ferret = stealth, agility, protection, healing

Fox = clever, cunning, intelligence, slyness, manipulator, attractiveness ("she's a fox"), camouflage, transformation, or psychic changes

Giraffe = stretching, risking ("sticking your neck out"), harmless curiosity, farsightedness, higher perspective

Goat = surefootedness, seeking new heights, determined, or cranky, blamed (scapegoat), stubborn, solitary

Groundhog = famous for Groundhog Day (February 2nd), watchful, options, many avenues of success, resilient, resourceful, a rich life

Guinea Pig = social, affection, trust, emotions, widen horizons, explore new possibilities, experiment, take risks, responsible, attentive, growth

Hamster = happiness, simple pleasures, small celebrations, bustling activity

Hippopotamus = weighty, ponderous, power, protection, or easily aroused, quick tempered, armored, impenetrable, resisting

Horse = progress, beauty, strength, power, travel, speed, vitality, free spirit

Hyena = instincts, or out of proportion noise and merriment, ferocious, sly

Jaguar = integrity, impeccability

Kangaroo = leap forward, mobility

Koala = calmness, relaxed

Leopard = power, strength, cunning, stealth, beauty, or revengeful, ruthless

Lion = courage, strength, fearlessness, bravery, royalty, leadership ("king of the jungle")

Llama = sure footed

Lynx = the unseen, hidden, secrets

Monkey= fun, playful, curiosity, activity, charm, communication, expression, subconscious activity, longevity, success, or malice, gossip

Moose= self-esteem

Mouse = timidity, fear, quiet, insignificant ("mousy"), poverty

Mule = stubborn, carrying a heavy burden

Opossum = appearances, diversion

Otter = joy, playfulness, sharing

Ox = effort

Panda = cuddly, lovable, tranquil, sensitivity

Panther = power

Penguin – pompous, pious, harmless, orthodox

Pig/Hog = selfish, greedy, gluttonous, overindulgence, inconsiderate

Polar Bear = powerful, teaching

Porcupine = innocence, protection, defense, or aggressive, belligerent, a prickly situation

Prairie Dog = family, affection, gregarious, community, social, teamwork, curiosity, alert, vigilance, retreat, health, healing

Rabbit = timidity, harmless, needs protection, fertility, abundance, or fear

Raccoon = industrious, dexterity, disguise, or mischief-maker

Rat = restlessness, shrewdness, success, or betrayer, wrongdoer, tattler ("ratting you out"), messy ("a rat's nest"), poverty, or vulgar, greed

Rhinoceros = power, forceful, charging ahead or impenetrable, extended egotism, ferocious temper

Sheep = the refusal or failure to think for oneself, misplaced trust, poor judgment, taken advantage of ("fleeced")

Skunk = respect, self-esteem, reputation, or penetrating odor ("something stinks"), violates good taste, wrong timing, protection

Sloth = wake up, get busy, regeneration, transformation, power, wisdom, sexuality, or danger,

Squirrel = frugality, preparations, activity, planning, stockpiling, storing, resourcefulness, communication, or hoarder or mischief-maker, gossip, selfishness

Tiger = strength, power, energy, devotion, or ruthless, destroying, devouring

Weasel = stealth, sly, secret

Wolf = powerful, friend, companion, guardian, loyalty, faithful, warm, spirit, teacher, hidden or cruel, cunning, greedy, relentless, revenge

Zebra = individuality, agility, success

U.S. OFFICIAL STATE MAMMALS

Most of the 50 U.S. states have an official representative mammal. Four have none, whereas other states have from two to six animals. Some states have both land and marine animals, some have wild and tame animals, and several have simply listed dogs and cats from rescue shelters. Similarly, Dr. Alberto Villoldo tells us, "countries have symbolic animals. The rooster is associated with France, the bear with Russia, and the panda with China. The eagle is the national symbol of at least eight countries, including the United States." The following compilation list is from several Internet websites:

Alabama = American black bear, Racking horse, West India manatee

Alaska = Moose, Bowhead whale, Alaskan Malamute dog

Arizona = Ring-tailed cat

Arkansas = White-tailed deer

California = California grizzly bear, California gray whale

Colorado = Rocky Mountain bighorn sheep, Rescue dogs and cats

Connecticut = Sperm whale

Delaware = Grey fox

District of Columbia = Manatee

Florida = Florida panther, Manatee, Porpoise, Florida cracker horse

Georgia = White-tailed deer, Right whale

Hawaii = Humpback whale, Hawaiian monk seal

Idaho = Appaloosa horse
Illinois = White-tailed deer
Indiana = (none)
Iowa = (none)

Kansas = American buffalo
Kentucky = Thoroughbred horse, Gray squirrel

Louisiana = Black bear, Louisiana Catahoula Leopard dog

Maine = Moose, Maine coon cat
Maryland = Calico cat, Chesapeake Bay retriever dog, Thoroughbred horse
Massachusetts = Tabby cat, Boston terrier, Morgan horse, Right whale
Michigan = White-tailed deer
Minnesota = (none)
Mississippi = White-tailed deer, Red fox, Bottle-nosed dolphin
Missouri = Missouri mule, Missouri Fox Trotting horse
Montana = Grizzly bear

Nebraska = White-tailed deer
Nevada = Desert Bighorn sheep
New Hampshire = White-tailed deer, Chinook dog, Bobcat
New Jersey = Horse
New Mexico = Black bear
New York = American beaver, Service dog
North Carolina = Grey squirrel
North Dakota = Plott hound dog, Colonial Spanish mustang, Virginia opossum, Nokota horse

Ohio = White-tailed deer
Oklahoma = Bison, Raccoon, White-tailed deer, Mexican free-tailed bat
Oregon = Beaver

Pennsylvania = White-tailed deer, Great dane dog
Rhode Island = (none)

South Carolina = White-tailed deer, Boykin spaniel dog, Bottle-nosed dolphin, Northern Right whale, Marsh tacky horse, Mule
South Dakota = Coyote

Tennessee = Tennessee walking horse, Raccoon, Rescue dogs and cats
Texas = Mexican free-tailed bat, Longhorn, 9-banded armadillo, Blue lacy dog, American quarter horse

Utah = Elk

Vermont = Morgan horse, Randall lineback cattle
Virginia = Virginia big-eared bat, American
  foxhound dog

Washington = Orca, Olympic marmot
West Virginia = Black bear
Wisconsin = Badger, American water spaniel dog,
  Dairy cow, White-tailed deer
Wyoming = Bison

Remember, the final authority of *meaning* is up
to you, the individual.

> *All symbols representing sentient or*
> *animal life are reverent.*
> —Ann Ree Colton

REPTILES & AMPHIBIANS

*Don't tell me you're an animal lover
if you only love the cute and fluffy.*
—Barry Goldsmith

Reptiles (snakes, lizards, turtles, crocodiles) and amphibians (frogs, toads, salamanders) are distantly related, and have certain qualities in common. They are all cold-blooded; their temperatures are affected by their surroundings. Their appearance and physical makeup differs; reptiles feel dry and scaly, whereas amphibians generally have smooth, moist or sticky skin. And they often live in different environments. The word amphibian means "double life" because they spend time in both the land and the water.

All too often, we overlook the many symbols and messages that surround us in our daily lives. In the case of reptiles and amphibians, many of us purposefully ignore their presence, thinking them "too icky" or "too yucky" to deal with. For example:

SIGNIFICANT INFLUENCE

I am not fond of snakes, in any way, shape, form, or fashion. The first time I dealt with a live snake, I was two years old, and didn't know anything about them. Mother was cooking, and my job was to go out into the garage, and get three potatoes, and bring them back. The potatoes were next to the garage wall in a long line. As I leaned down to pick one up, there was an equally long snake, staring at me. What a shock! I screamed bloody murder, and both my parents rushed out of the house, as did all our local neighbors, who stood at a respectful distance in a wide semi-circle behind us. The second shock was that my father had been shaving in the bathroom, and had charged out of the house in his undershorts. The third shock was when he grabbed a huge stick and immediately began to wildly fight the snake, bashing it to smithereens. He was a country boy, having grown up around snakes on his family farm, and therefore knew a poisonous snake when he saw one. So nakedness, violence, death, and snakes became all mixed up in my tiny mind.

Nor did movies help, as I got older. I vividly remember the scene in *True Grit*, starring John Wayne and Glen Campbell, where the girl falls in a mine shaft, and is surrounded by snakes; and that of *Alexander* (the Great), wherein he (Colin Farrell) is talking to his mother (Angelina Jolie) in her room, with about a hundred snakes undulating around on the floor. Ugh! And tales of Medusa didn't help either. So the less I heard of snakes, the better.

CLASSROOM MAYHEM

One year, as a specialist, I was to help a 5th grade teacher. Each day, I had to hold my nose, and gear myself up, to enter her room. She had cages of animals everywhere, and they weren't kept clean. The smell was atrocious, and it was hard to keep from gagging. She had two huge snakes, which she named King Tut and Cleopatra. In my building, a hamster had somehow found a way out of its cage, and it could have been anywhere within seven adjoining classrooms in the building. When the 5th grade teacher heard about the missing hamster, she grabbed King Tut, ran over to my room's door, opened it, and threw King Tut inside, yelling, "King Tut will find it!" All I could think of was that if the snake did find the hamster, he would probably *eat it!* I couldn't believe what I had just witnessed, and when I entered my classroom, my roommate specialist was standing on top of the table, freaking out. I thought she was dancing and putting on a show for my benefit, and I was laughing at her antics, until I focused on her face—her eyes were as big as saucers—and realized that she was truly alarmed! Oh, boy. So I wasn't the only one that had a problem with snakes!

PET SNAKE

Obviously, I didn't pass my fears onto my sons. After my oldest son was married, he and his wife became enamored with snakes, and kept some as pets. One day, they came over to visit, and he had a long, slender snake wrapped around his neck. They had just come from shopping, where he also wore it into stores, causing scenes here and there. Another shock to my system.

SNAKE DREAM

While working on this chapter—with reptiles and amphibians uppermost on my mind—I had a dream, which has bothered me no end. I was walking down the street toward home, when on the corner lawn, next to the curb, were seven snakes stretched out lengthwise, with four more in the overhanging tree. All were big and long, and different. Most appeared to be unmoving, whereas some were still slightly twitching. I freaked, and ran home, to call the Animal Control to come and do something about all the snakes. The man who lives in the corner house, often goes camping in the desert, so once I calmed down, I thought that he must have caught them, for some reason or other. When I awoke, I was upset to have seen *eleven* snakes in my dream. Historically, I know that snake symbolism has many positive attributes, and I know that the numbers four is a solid number, and seven, and eleven are auspicious numbers. But I can't get past my early conditioning. So I'm ignoring the negative snake symbolism, and am focusing solely upon the positive and the numbers. Baby steps.

*We have a lot to be thankful
to reptiles for,
not the least of which is
their control of rodents.*
—Romulus Whitaker

According to the Internet, there are 8,240 reptile species, and approximately 10,000 amphibian species worldwide. The following compilation list of common reptiles and amphibians—and the significant meanings involved—is offered via Andrews, Arruda, Colton, Eisenbraun, Hallberg, Harris, Linn, the MacGregors, Upczak. and Venefica. Use the list for dream interpretation, or for understanding the symbolism of the reptile or amphibian that has unexpectedly appeared in your life:

REPTILES & AMPHIBIAN SYMBOLOGY

Alligator = primal/ancient power, survival, instinct, wisdom, hidden, patience, protection, speed, strength, grounded, new opportunities, new beginnings, healing, or fear

Chameleon = flexibility, adaptability, camouflage, dramatic change, new opportunities, strong clairvoyance, add color to your life

Crocodile = strength, power, wisdom, balance, trust, or trouble, danger, dishonesty ("crocodile tears"), hypocrisy ("it's a crock"), viciousness, fury, destruction

Frog = fertility, change, new beginnings, opportunities, explore, creative voice, productive, patience, focus, change, or finding beauty beneath surface

Gecko = strife, stress, conflict, insight, action, objectivity, proper response, detachment, safety

Iguana = simplify life, climb new goals

Lizard = camouflage, observant, important dreams, subconscious mind

Newt = new ideas, inspirations, creative endeavors, successful ventures, express artistic side

Salamander = self-examination, strong psychic sensitivity, changes, assistance, cooperation, success

Scorpion = unexpected offence,

Snake = healing; shedding yourself of relationships, beliefs, and situations, ("a snake in the grass"), wisdom, fertility, sexual energy ("one-eyed snake"—male genitalia), personal growth, rebirth, transformation, healing opportunities, creative life force, manifestation, guidance, positive change, the umbilical cord joining all humans to Mother Earth, immortality, or lying ("speaking with a forked tongue"), strong unconscious energies, frightening dreams, temptation, danger, poisonous defensiveness, vengefulness, vindictiveness, and death.

Toad = skills, resources, trust inner strength

Tortoise = burdens, changes, facing obstacles and moving on, slow and steady progress, do not force matters, opportunities, withdrawal from problems, plodding

Worm = hidden preparation, works beneath the surface, or lowlife, no backbone ("worming in")

> *Reptiles and amphibians are*
> *sometimes thought of as*
> *primitive, dull and dimwitted.*
> *In fact, of course, they can be*
> *lethally fast,*
> *spectacularly beautiful,*
> *surprisingly affectionate,*
> *and very sophisticated.*
> —Sir David Attenborough

SPIDERS, INSECTS, & SUCH

*If you think you're too small
to make a difference,
try going to bed with a mosquito.*
—Anita Roddick

"People with small minds do not see the limitless adventures and boundless knowledge that tiny insects have to offer. And people with big minds have the ability to be humble in the presence of a small insect," so say Steven R. Kutcher (steven@bugsaremybusiness.com) and Barrett Klein.

Insects have a three-part body, six jointed-legs, wings, compound eyes, and antennae. Included within the same group are archnids, which are wingless, with no antennae, having a two-part body, and eight jointed-legs (spiders, scorpions, ticks, mites, and Daddy Longlegs), and arthropods, which have an exoskeleton, a segmented body, and jointed appendages (centipedes, millipedes, sow bugs, pill bugs, potato bugs). The latter two sets of critters are not really insects, nor are worms and snails, but most people lump them altogether, as pests, under the popular heading of "creepy crawlers."

A number of my friends totally freak out upon seeing a spider, whereas I find them to be utterly fascinating. I see spiders in my house on a daily basis, and joyfully watch over them. When I know that visitors or the housekeepers are coming, I carefully remove the spiders, and take them outside, bidding them a happy life elsewhere. I agree with the old American Quaker saying: "If you want to live and thrive, let the spider run alive."

To me, spiders are associated with spiral energy, creativity, and linking the past to the future. I think of the spiders I see as descendants of the Hopi's Spider Woman, and other Native American tribes' Grandmother Spider, as well as the Hindus' Indra's Net, and India's Maya, the weaver of illusions. I harken back to the Greek myth of Arachne, and the West African and Caribbean tales of Anansi (which literally means spider). So, what my friends and I think about spiders, and the way we treat spiders, are two different things entirely.

SPIDERS

> I read the classic children's book, *Charlotte's Web*, by E.B. White, to my third graders every single year. They all loved that book. Afterward, I presented many follow-up science lessons about spiders. It was so gratifying to see the

pupils change their attitudes (from being deathly *afraid* of spiders, to being open and knowledgeable about them; from not caring about the natural world, to nurturing and protecting nature). They would carefully remove spiders from the classroom, in little paper cups, or call me to have the honor of placing spiders on the outside hedges. It was wonderful to see this reverence for life. One year, an elderly woman became an aide in my classroom. During a quiet time of individual assignments, she spied a spider meandering down an aisle. "Watch out! *A Spider!*" she shrieked, as—SPLAT!—she stomped on it. The room became so deathly still, you would have thought that everyone had suffered a heart attack in unison. Oh, woe!

I had the same problem with my own children's book, *The Cockroach Invasion*. No adult professional artists wanted to deal with the topic, even though it was a true story, that actually happened in my third grade classroom. So I finally had an art contest for children, and the 19 winning sketches are scattered throughout the book. Children loved the topic, whereas their parents were extremely upset or agitated by the very thought of cockroaches. Adults would shiver in reaction. One neighbor told me, in frantic mode, that she couldn't get past the cover, as it was so scary. Another neighbor told me that there was no way she could read such a book, and I laughed and told her not to worry; that the book was given to her for her *grandchildren*. I had some great responses, and very funny experiences, as a result of getting the story published. The attitude change in adults was a wonder to behold. Now, several years later, adults still want to talk about it. My dentist, and his staff, are now naming any cockroaches they see. What a riot!

Understand that nothing is too small or insignificant to bring a message to you:

UNANTICIPATED RESULT

"That little bug isn't going to hurt you!" I announced in my most judgmental voice, as the third graders were quickly shifting their positions to get out of its way. We had been sitting in a circle on the rug, quietly reading our textbooks, when a beautiful, iridescent, emerald-green beetle (the likes of which I had never seen, before or since), arrived out of nowhere to interrupt our lesson. It irritated me that such a little insect, the size and shape of a ladybug, could command so much attention, even if it *did* move in such a speedy fashion.

No sooner had I made this unfounded statement than the bug circled around and made a beeline straight at me. It leaped upon my ankle and bit me, before I could even attempt to move— CRUNCH!— and the pain came in Technicolor.

Immediately, my ankle and foot swelled to such unbelievable proportions that it became difficult to pry off my shoe. The infected area was beet-red, hot to the touch, and started to throb with a rhythm roughly approximating the speed and intensity of a jungle drum. After school, I hobbled over—with one shoe off and one shoe on—to see the nurse, who gave me a list of addresses of specific doctors to see on my way home. (Naturally, one doctor was on vacation, and another—situated clear across town in the opposite direction— had moved. It took me quite a while to find a doctor who was on the list, and, because I didn't have an appointment, I had to wait for a good length of time to see him.

Suffice it to say that I was out of commission for *three* days, taking anti-venom shots, and swallowing anti-inflammatory pills. As a result, this experience taught the children NOT to believe everything a teacher says, and I learned to keep my mouth shut about things I know nothing about. Needless to say, this was a very painful lesson for me to learn, both figuratively and literally.

DIVE BOMBERS

And then, there was the time when three summer classes went to the El Dorado Nature Center. The students had congregated at the building to tour the exhibits. Unexpectedly, bees from a nearby hive dive-bombed everyone! In a split second, the air was full of tiny yellow bodies, and cries of pain. Children charged off every which way, some with five or six welts each, and other without any, but everyone hysterical, nonetheless. Needless to say, all were preoccupied with bee stings, and little other learning took place that afternoon. It was the perfect time, however, for creative writing, and to introduce Rimsky-Korsakov's "Flight of the Bumble Bee" for music appreciation. Imagination soared! The following day, the class compared and contrasted said piece of music with that of B. Bumble and the Stinger's "Bumble Boogie." The students loved it! Ah, timing! (Any experience can become a lesson.)

FIGHTING FLEAS

My son and I went to the movies, to see the first Rocky movie, that everyone had been talking about. It was a pretty new theater within the Los Cerritos Mall complex. The place was packed. But we couldn't concentrate on the movie, because huge fleas were bombarding us. The whole time Rocky was fighting on the screen, we were fighting in our seats. I finally caught one, and held it between my thumb and pointer finger. I went out into the lobby, to speak to the manager. He looked all of sixteen years old, and couldn't empathize with our situation. Nor did he want to see the giant flea that I was holding in my hand. I was not satisfied with his response, so I held the flea all the way home. Then I wrote a scathing letter to the local Health Department site, and scotch-taped the flea to the top of the letter. They called me in response, saying it was a pretty new facility (only about three years old), and I said that I knew that, and couldn't believe it either. I told them exactly where we sat, and they checked it out. It must have been really bad, because the theater was closed down for two weeks, while it was being fumigated. Whereupon, my son and I danced a victory dance to the Rocky theme song.

POINT OF VIEW

When presenting the homework assignment to my senior citizen's creative writing class, I was trying to describe the villains they had known. "You know, the potato bugs in your lives."

"Yuck!"

"Disgusting!"

"Eeeyu!" was the overwhelming response, as they grimaced, and talked over one another. They all had a story.

One woman, however, took another view entirely. She found potato bugs to be fascinating. We all shuddered and groaned. But she adamantly stood her ground, to the point that I went

directly home, and researched them. At
length. I still find potato bugs to be icky
("Satan's fetus," or "The Devil's spawn"
as one country calls them), but it was
refreshing to see them from her point
of view.

It is estimated that the U.S. has 91,000 described insect species, with an added undescribed number of 73,000. Yikes! Recent 2012 figures (according to serpentspeaks.windpress.com) indicated that there are more than 200 million insects for each human on the planet, or 300 pounds of insects for every pound of humans. Yousers! It is estimated that there are 10 quitillion (10,000,000,000.000,000,000) individual insects alive at this very moment. And the National Pest Management Association says that "The termites on earth outweigh the humans on earth!"

The following short compilation list of insects, archnids, and arthropods—with their significant meanings—is offered via Andrews, Arruda, Colton, Hallberg, Linn, the MacGregors, Upczak. and Venefica. Use this list for dream interpretation, or for understanding the symbolism of the insect that has unexpectedly appeared in your life:

INSECT SYMBOLOGY

Ant = busy, industrious, productive, disciplined, effort, community, cooperation, or restless, antsy, workaholic

Bee = work, industrious, order, cooperation, diligence, generosity, buzzing network of communication, teamwork, sweetness, treasure, action fertility, royalty

Beetle = good luck, joy, resurrection, eternal life, renewal

Butterfly = transformation, profound changes, new beginnings, soul, rebirth, resurrection, joy, ride the winds of changes

Bug = annoyance, inconvenience

Caterpillar = possibilities, unharnessed potential, transformation, good luck, new birth

Centipede = psychic movement, connecting with spirit, psychic protection

Cicada = change, renewal, rebirth, happiness, longevity, patience, shift in energy, timing

Cricket = peace, joy, long life, happiness, sensitive intuition, blessings, protector, power of belief

Cockroach = adaptability, instincts, perseverance, determination, virtually indestructible, survival, or distasteful, lack of emotions and thought, sensitive to change (Terri Guillemets once declared: "Cockroaches really put my 'all creatures great and small' creed to the test.")

Daddy Longlegs = harmony, balance, success in endeavors, hope, new understanding, creativity, ideas, deep relationships, surprises, greater vision

Dragonfly = change, transformation, communication, wisdom, understanding dreams, enlightenment, good news, good luck, or illusions

Firefly = search for truth, hope, energy, attraction, new ideas, awakening, spiritual inspiration, awakening to spirit, guidance, radiance, illumination

Flea = irritating, agitating, disturbing, make necessary changes

Fly = small annoyance, pest, infectious, a spreader of malice, spy, movement, troublesome issues, tend to your responsibilities, a need for stability, perspective, act quickly, vision, or (Ogden Nash once said, "God in His wisdom made the fly, and then forgot to tell us why."). evo;,satanic

Glow worm = "let your light shine" (Someone once observed: "A glow worm's never glum. "Cuz how can you be grumpy, when the sun shines out your bum?")

Grasshopper = living for the moment, fun, an unsettled mind, unable to concentrate, uncanny leaps forward, many together are a plague or a curse

Hornet = unwelcome, stirring up trouble, aggravating

June Bug = higher intuition, judges well in all areas, pay attention to synchronicities

Ladybug = good luck, happiness, wishes fulfilled, abundance, protection, tend to your home and family ("Ladybug, Ladybug, fly away home"), transformation, well being, joy. or pushing too hard, be patient

Leech = cleansing, purification, detoxification, healing, let joy unfold

Lice = contamination, incestuous

Mosquito = annoying, irritation, persistent, attacks, negative thoughts, unsolved issues, many mosquitos mean many enemies (Someone once asked: "Why didn't Noah swat those two mosquitoes?" And Andy Warhol once observed, "The mosquito is the state bird of New Jersey.")

Moth = perseverance beyond reason; something eating away at you, fertility, relations, sexual activity

Praying Mantis = camouflage, silence, stillness, vision, swift, deliberate, precise, action

Scorpion = foreboding, defensiveness, stinging protection, negative, transformation, secrets, passion, desire

Slug = stretching oneself to incredible lengths, trust, follows the trails of others, or slow, lazy, sluggard, no shortcuts

Snail = home, protection, keep your guard up, travel, safety, self reliance, or vulnerable, moving slowly ("at a snail's pace")

Spider = strength, powerful creativity, cunning, good luck, patience, amazing insight and assistance, go directly to the center of whatever you are dealing with, or manipulation, deception ("web of illusion")

Stick bug = patience, camouflage, hiding, activity beneath the surface

Termites = erosion caused by negativity, and irresponsibility, undermining a situation or person

Tick = unbalanced relationships

Wasp = practical, responsible role, efforts and dreams fulfilled, independence, self-sufficiency, or jealous, revengeful, antisocial, hostile

Worm = working old ground, examine and digest life, open to new growth, get fresh air, face reality, hope

Two-legged creatures we are supposed to love
as we love ourselves.
The four-legged, also seem to be pretty important.
But six legs are too many
from the human standpoint.
—Joseph W. Krutch

BIRDS

A bird does not sing
because it has an answer.
It sings because
it has a song.
—Chinese Proverb

"Everyone likes birds," Sir David Attenborough said. "What wild creature is more accessible to our eyes and ears, or close to us and everyone in the world, as universal as a bird?" As such, they are common spiritual symbols. Indeed, as the MacGregors tell us, birds are tuned into their surroundings, and recognize those people who are dealing with intense situations and high emotion, and are able to comfort them, in one way or another.

And, as Chopra has noted (as well as you and I have), several birds, or a large flock of birds, move in harmony with each other, without an obvious leader. "They change direction in an instant, all birds altering their course at the exact same moment, and they do it perfectly. You never see birds bumping into each other in flight. They climb, and turn, and swoop so that they look like a single organism, as if some unspoken command was issued that they all obeyed at once." Onlookers often wonder how that happens. Chopra continues: "The complexity and absolute precision of the birds' behavior stumps physical science every time."

Birds are often associated with synchronicities. Throughout ancient times to the present, birds have been considered as both symbols and omens. Through augury, people have been receptive to the messages birds bring, interpreting their movements and flight patterns. (As a child, I always used birds as forecasters of events, and considered bird locations or flight positions—up down, right or left, fast or slow, a single bird or a flock—as good or bad signals or signs. I never knew that anyone else had ever done so. I figured that it was my little secret.)

Birds are symbols of freedom, soaring, good news, joy, and wisdom. They represent transition and the future. Only a few specific species are considered ill omens. If birds are caged, it is symbolic of your lack of freedom. Note that symbolism varies between regions and cultures.

GOOD INTENTIONS

I was concerned about Hallelujah, one of my best third graders that year. He was clearly upset. Several times during the hour he came up to me, to whisper his grief about his pet bird that had died that morning. Thinking to console him, I rummaged through stacks of my personal children's books, and finally found *The Tenth Good Thing About Barney*, by Judith Viorst. The book is about a little boy whose cat had died. I thought it might help Hallelujah to see how another youngster had handled a similar loss.

Later in the day, after I had presented a lesson about continents, and everyone was involved in the map follow-up assignment, Hallelujah came up to me, and slammed the book on my desk. "Well, I read it," he announced, "but I didn't like it!"

"But, *why*?" I asked, thoroughly shaken, while mentally flogging myself for my good intentions.

"Because it was sad, and it's too much like what happened to me," he explained. "You know, Ms. Meinberg," he continued softly, "everyone has been so *nice* to me today. And everyone has tried so hard to cheer me up. But, you know, I just can't be happy today, no matter what. *It's just too soon!*"

I marveled at the wisdom of this child. I don't like to recall how many years it took me to discover that time, does indeed, heal all wounds.

BIRD NEST

After playing on the Giant Eucalyptus Tree (mentioned earlier), the third graders began jumping over the bushes that the storm had left in its wake. Eventually, they dragged the bushes together, to form a gigantic circle, which they called their "nest." In their fantasy play, they became birds that lived in the nest, and they played happily at this for a while. Then they all "flew" over to where I was sitting (chirping and wildly flapping their arms), and begged me to become a part of their bird play. It was a beautiful way to leave the park that day: as a *family*.

There are approximately 10,000 bird species in the world. The following short compilation list of common birds—and their significant meanings—is offered via Andrews, Arruda, Colton, Hallberg, Linn, the MacGregors, Mascarenhas, Upczak. and Venefica. Use this list for dream interpretation, or for understanding the symbolism of the bird that has unexpectedly appeared in your life:

BIRD SYMBOLOGY

Albatross = omens, success, or burdens

Blackbird = a good omen, socialize, creativity, heightened psychic awareness, mystical, magical or vulnerable, a lack of confidence, shyness, insecurity

Bluebirds = happy, contented, innocence, joy, transitions, arrival of spring, hard work, spiritual awakenings

Blue jay = faithful, purity, adaptable, clarity, fearless, truthful, talkative

Buzzard = scavenger, clean up, loose ends

Canary = happiness, joy, spread well-being, intellectual development, or gossip, and since canaries used to be used in the mines—to provide an early warning system of dangerous gasses—this might be a signal of impending danger, a problem, or an unpleasant situation

Cardinal = beauty, vibrancy, vitality, nobility, love, warmth, or self- importance

Chickadee = cheerful, expression, clarity, purity of soul, higher thinking, better understanding, happy, fearless, truthful, faithful

Chicken = timidity, cowardice, lack of self esteem, not logical, fearful ("chicken-hearted", "chickened out") or fertility, protectiveness, sacrifice

Cockatoo = courtship. relationship bonds

Condor = overcoming limitations, ancient mysteries, life and death, spirit communication

Crane = peaceful, healing, renewal, rejuvenation, change old ways or patterns, longevity, honor, justice, prosperity, beauty, stamina, communicate clearly, focus

Crow = messenger, great knowledge, straight talker, perception, a portent of change, creativity, mystical powers, or arrogant, boastful, cunning, materialistic, mischievous, bandit, trickster, illusions, malicious gossip (The MaGregors say:"Esoterically, crows are associated with battlefields, medieval hospitals, execution sites, and cemeteries.")

Cuckoo = silly, unrealistic, new fate

Dove = peace, love, purity, innocence, spirituality, spirit, hope, gentleness, the Holy Ghost, spirit messenger, communication, maternity, femininity, prophecy

Duck = migrator, simplicity, honesty, or aggressiveness

Eagle = freedom, power, action, speed, daring, courage, stamina, resilience, honesty, truthfulness, perception, loner, creative, leader, higher perspective ("seeing the bigger picture"; "the bird's eye view"), prosperity, generosity, kindness, triumph, confidence, renewal, royalty, faith, healing, peace, enlightenment, messenger, reach for the sky, seeker, visionary, challenges, a massive life change, mystical attainment, loyal affairs, divine, spirit, illumination

Falcon = hope, help coming to you, family-oriented, spirituality, freedom

Finch = variety, multiplicity

Flamingo = beauty, balance, grace, responsibility, leadership, messenger cleansing, healing, flighty, flirtations, community, lessons of the heart or obsolete situation

Goose = silly, foolish, foolish, quarrelsome, babbler, watchful, swift response, naïve, blind faith, travel, or seeing a flight of geese in a V-shaped formation is a sign of victory

Gulls = responsible behavior, communication

Hawk = messenger, persistent, visionary power, guardianship, inspiration, grace, agility, logical, honest, truthful. a broader perspective, or destroyer

Heron = calmness, patience, determination, contented, self-reliant, reasoning, a good omen, leader, longevity

Hummingbird = joy, beautiful, messenger, optimistic, devotion, positivity, infinity, healing, energy, nectar of life. Because hummingbirds navigate thousands of miles in their grand immigration from

Canada to Brazil, they also represent long-distance travel, an epic journey, sense of direction, persistence, pressing forward, tireless activity, hope, insight, wisdom, messenger

Ibis = scavenger, deadly deeds

Kingfisher = beauty, agility, speed, peaceful, success, prosperity, faithfulness

Lark = harmony, luck, awakening

Loon = hopes, wishes, lucid dreaming, reawakening

Macaw = vibrant, psychic, intelligent, balance, resourceful, well-adjusted vision, spiritual perception, healing, new light

Magpie = intelligence, occult knowledge

Meadowlark = cheerful, inner journey

Mockingbird = recognition of abilities, finding your soul purpose, or imitation, mockeryNightingale = love and longing, charity, good omen, creative, transformation, or warning, an impending death

Oriole = joy, warms

Ostrich = insensitive, foolish, shy, evasive ("head in the sands"), prideful

Owl = transformation, vigilance, learning, knowledge, wisdom, an omen during times of passage and transition, accomplishment, magic, patience, enlightenment, or being judged, danger, ill omen, doom, deception, a harbinger of death

Parakeet = joyful, curiosity, chatter without saying much

Parrot = jungle, color, expression, mimicking other's words, imitators, dependent on others for views, opinions, and ideas, or a gossiper, someone making fun of you

Peacock = beauty, confidence, vanity, or pride ("pride goeth before a fall"), or resurrection

Pelican = abundance, charity, generosity, unselfishness

Penguin = lucid dreaming, astral projection

Pheasant = sexuality, fertility, harmony. spiritual seeker, or going astray, seduction, secrecy, wickedness

Pigeon = youthful, ignorance, determined, overcomes obstacles, safest in a flock, community, communication, home, family, security, love, or blaming, gossiping, dirty pests

Quail = group harmony, family oriented, lust and love, protective, victory over obstacles, or too trusting, secrets, fear, recoil, dread

Raven = magic, shape-shifting, good omen, alertness, watchfulness, teacher, inward journey, a big change, or misfortune, deception, can predict death and disease

Roadrunner = mental speed, agility, fast, great reflexes, quick thinker, well adjusted, leadership

Robin = new ideas, new beginnings, new opportunities, growth, rebirth

Sandpiper = quick wit, adventurous spirit, explorer, focused, foraging

Seagulls = intelligent, messenger, skillful

Sparrow = sweet, gentle, hope, intelligent, fertility, renewal, awakening, nobility

Starling = etiquette, group behavior

Stork = fertility, birth, new arrival, rejuvenation, creativity, philosophy, new project, happiness, contentment, good luck, in folklore: storks deliver babies

Swallow = protection, home, warmth, love, perspective, discipline, rejuvenation, spring

Swan = beauty, elegance, grace, purity, innocence, romance, faithfulness (they mate for life), honesty, integrity, spiritual awakening, freedom, perfection or altered states of awareness, development of the mind; spiritual transition

Swift = speed, agility

Toucan = companionship, partnership, teamwork, peace, relaxation, or impending death

Turkey = sacrifice, selflessness, healing after surgery, spiritual rejuvenation, or restlessness

Vulture = greedy, demonic approach to life, impending gloom. death or they can show how to make good out of bad, and life out of death

Woodpecker = protection, guardian of trees, industrious, prophetic, mystic powers, signals rain and storm

Wren = boldness, resourcefulness

OFFICIAL U.S. NATIONAL BIRD

The American Bald Eagle was chosen to be the emblem of the United States of America, in 1782. It was selected as the national bird because of its great strength, long life, and majestic looks. Because it flies higher than any other bird, it represents unlimited freedom. It encourages onlookers not to settle for the status quo, but to stretch one's limits by reaching beyond; to look at things from a higher perspective. (And it was erroneously believed to exist only on this continent.) And all 50 states U.S. states have an official bird.

OFFICIAL U.S. STATE BIRDS

Alabama = Northern Flicker/Wild Turkey
Alaska = Willow Ptarmigan
Arizona = Cactus Wren
Arkansas = Mockingbird

California = California Valley Quail
Colorado = Lark Bunting
Connecticut = American Robin

Delaware = Blue He Chicken
District of Columbia = Wood Thrush

Florida = Mockingbird

Georgia = Brown Thrasher/Bobwhite Quail

Hawaii = Nene

Idaho = Mountain Bluebird/Peregrine Falcon
Illinois = Northern Cardinal
Indiana = Northern Cardinal
Iowa = Eastern Goldfinch

Kansas = Western Meadowlark
Kentucky = Northern Cardinal

Louisiana = Brown Pelican

Maine = Black-capped Chickadee

Maryland = Baltimore Oriole
Massachusetts = Black-capped Chickadee/Wild
    Turkey
Michigan = Robin Redbreast
Minnesota = Common Loon
Mississippi = Wood Duck/Mockingbird
Missouri = Bobwhite Quail/Eastern Quail
Montana = Western Meadowlark
Nebraska = Western Meadowlark
Nevada = Mountain Bluebird
New Hampshire = Purple Finch
New Jersey = Eastern Goldfinch
New Mexico = Greater Roadrunner
New York = Eastern Bluebird
North Carolina = Northern Cardinal
North Dakota = Western Meadowlark

Ohio = Northern Cardinal
Oklahoma = Scissor-tailed Flycatcher/Wild Turkey
Oregon = Western Meadowlark

Pennsylvania = Ruffed Grouse

Rhode Island = Rhode Island Red

South Carolina = Wild Turkey
South Dakota = Ring-necked Pheasant

Tennessee = Mockingbird/Bobwhite Quail
Texas = Mockingbird

Utah = California Gull

Vermont = Hermit Thrush
Virginia= Northern Cardinal

Washington = Willow Goldfinch
West Virginia = Northern Cardinal
Wisconsin = American Robin/Mourning Dove
Wyoming = Western Meadowlark

American Samoa = Moa/Manumea (not officially
   recognized)
Guam = Guam Rail
Northern Marianas = Mariana Fruit-Dove
Puerto Rico = Puerto Rico Spindalis
U.S. Virgin Islands = Bananaquit

> *You can know the name of a bird in all the*
> *languages of the world, but when you're finished,*
> *you'll know absolutely nothing*
> *whatsoever about the bird . . .*
> *So let's look at the bird and see what it's doing—*
> *that's what counts.*
> *—Richard Feynman*

SEA LIFE

The world's finest wilderness
lies beneath the waves.
—Robert Wyland

A major proportion of all life lives in the ocean. It is not known the extent of the percentage since many of the species are still to be discovered. Marine life is a vast resource for humans, providing food, medicine, jobs, recreation, and tourism. Fish and sea life symbolism commonly represent independence, potential, and possibilities.

UP CLOSE AND PERSONAL

My husband and two sons, Danny (age 13), and Jay (age 6), were fishing on the beach one night, in the ocean waters of Seal Beach, California. They were fishing for barred perch. The grunion were running at the same time, so many people were walking around with their flashlights, or wading in the surf. Everyone was killing time, simply waiting for the grunion to run. Danny hooked a leopard shark—a female, over five feet long—and brought her in. It was apparent that she was pregnant, so they treated her gently. The boys dug along trench in the sand, and placed a huge plastic tarp along the bottom, and they filled the trench with buckets of water. Then the three of them gently carried the shark, and carefully laid her in the long trench.

The boys placed their Coleman lanterns around the area, so people could see how beautiful the shark was, with spots like a leopard. It was the first time most visitors had ever seen a live shark, and much oohing and ahhing took place. Everyone had many questions about the shark (How big are its teeth? What does it eat? and so forth), which both boys happily answered. They were excited to share what they knew. It was enjoyable to hear their confident replies, and watch their interactions with the crowd. Although young, they were already seasoned fishermen.

When my husband was asked, "Where was it caught?", he pointed straight out to the ocean surf. No one could believe that they were wading in the same foam in which the shark had been swimming. They were further astounded to find that she was also waiting for the grunion, as were other species of sharks (shovel-nosed and gray sharks), alongside cow-nosed rays, yellow- fin croakers, corbina, and small stingrays, that stayed a little further off-shore.

The boys frequently changed the water for the leopard shark. Some of the more adventurous visitors wanted to touch her, and were totally amazed that she left like sandpaper. People learned a lot from the boys, who were excited to share their knowledge (which warmed the cockles of my teacher heart, as you may well imagine).

Later, the three of them together tenderly lifted the leopard shark, and carried her back into the ocean, where she peacefully swam away. This impromptu hands-on experience turned two youngsters into unexpected teachers, and visitors of all ages into learners. *How fun it that?!*

CRITTER LOVER

One eight-year-old was a loner. He did not know how to relate to other children. He was only comfortable with animals. He played hookey often, and the office staff could usually find him in a meadow, down by the railroad tracks, looking for animals. He always brought his "friends" to school with him. Every time I stuck my hand in his desk —a feat of bravery that I considered second only to rushing a machine gun nest— something new would pop out (a rabbit, a grasshopper, crickets, butterflies, moths, lizards, frogs, toads, worms, as well as a huge cockroach with a long thread leash). I was always afraid that I would be greeted with a snake one day. I finally solved the problem, by placing his desk next to my 26- gallon aquarium, where the fish had a decidedly calming effect on him.

According to the Census of Marine Life, over 17,000 species thrive deep in the ocean where no light penetrates. As far as how many species live by the shore, estimates differ from 178,000 to more than 10 million. So who can even begin to estimate how many species are in the ocean as a whole? Especially when scientists say that there are 38,000 different kinds of microbes in a liter of seawater. Talk about diversity! The mind boggles.

The following short compilation list of the more commonly known sea life—and their significant meanings—is offered via Andrews, Arruda, Colton, Hallberg, Linn, the MacGregors, Upczak, and Venefica). Use this list for dream interpretation, or for understanding the symbology of the sea creature that has unexpectedly appeared in your life:

SEA LIFE SYMBOLOGY

Barnacle = coexisting, latching on, free ride

Barracuda = highly aggressive, ambush, action, strength, courage, danger, predator, power, speed, vicious

Clam = not cooperating, materialistic, secretive, retreat

Crab = escapist, scuttling sideways, bad mood, hidden and protected

Dolphin = friend, love, joy, playfulness, spontaneity, harmony, intelligence, mental telepathy, transformation, spirituality, enlightenment

Fish = spirituality, fertility wealth, riches, food, subconscious, or sounds a bit off ("fishy" or a "red herring")

Flying fish = emotionally free, uninhibited

Goldfish = peace, abundance, prosperity, harmony

Jellyfish = spineless, floating or drifting, organization, cooperation, success

Lobster = independence, solitude, seclusion, protection, strength, cycles, regenerate, rejuvenation, transformation, deepest emotions, emotional growth, good fortune, luxury, wealth, prosperity, longevity

Manatee = gentle, slow and steady, remove old emotional baggage, deliberately move forward, be open, easy-going, trusting, wide range of possibilities, or passiveness, lazy, lacks ambition and drive.
a touch of sadness

Narwhal = power, luck, romance, love, money, success, creativity, talented, wisdom, freedom, "the unicorn of the sea", wonder, fantasy, imagination, deeper awareness, subconscious, universal truths

Nautilus = beauty, camouflage, safe, comfortable

Octopus = intelligent, agility, grace, flexibility, creativity, adaptability, stealth, camouflage, free-moving, shy, retiring, defense, cut loose excess baggage, regeneration, mystic center, good memories, eight is a power number

Orca = intelligent, problem-solving, cooperative, team member, faithful (mates for life), intuition, submerged emotions, longevity

Oyster = sensitive, simple, quiet, toughness, strength, balance. protection, inner self, hidden treasure, peaceful, harmonious, triumph over adversity

Porpoise = knowledge, wisdom, change, balance, harmony, freedom, joy, trust, healing

Pufferfish = mellow unless provoked, prefers family and friends to new people, wide-ranging intellect, insightful, kind, helpful, or prickly, sometimes poisonous

Sand dollar = transformation, strength, protection, bravery, freedom, social, success

Sea anemone = good luck, beautiful, receptive, protection from enemies

Sea coral = bravery, wisdom, success, modesty, happiness, reduces stress and fears, immortality

Sea cucumber = good health or being restored to good health happiness, friendliness, playfulness, creativity, good fortune, healing

Seahorse = unique, mystical, calm, strength, power, mild-mannered, contentment, patient, good luck, romance, creativity, productive, responsibility, or inflexibility, stubborn

Seal = intelligent, creative, imagination, balance, dreams, playfulness, inquisitiveness, closure on something ("seal the deal"), prosperity, good luck, success

Sea lion = wealth, abundance, prosperity, cleverness, playfulness, imaginative, creativity, good luck, success

Sea otter = a marine mammal that spends most of its life in the water, childlike, accept what is, seek out the joy of the moment, lighten up,

Sea shells = love, fertility, intuition, sensitivity, imagination, creativity, clarity, insight, transformation, expresses emotions and ideas, healing

Sea turtle = inner wisdom, blessings, intuition, persevere, trust, move forward, vast journeys, self-pacing, patience, protection, longevity

Sea worms = negative forces within

Shark = danger, terror, violence, power, predator, relentless, fearlessness

Shrimp = small, overlooked, underestimated, feeling inferior or unimportant, scavenger

Squid = Overwhelmed, going in many directions at once, camouflage, devouring, Can red the moods and body language of others, using light, color, and form to communicate.

Starfish = unique, healing, regeneration, renewing, guidance, intuition, connection, inspiration, brilliance

Stingray = graceful, smooth, staying on course, never lost, confident, trust abilities

Swordfish = virtue, courage, strength

Walrus = social-minded, slow-thinking, or pompous

Whale = maneuverability, Record Keeper, perception, intuition, gentle, nonaggressive, power, strength, size ("a whale of a job")

> *Marine organisms do not care about*
> *international boundaries;*
> *they move where they will.*
> —Paul Snelgrove

NUMBERS

*Numbers constitute the
only universal language.*
—Nathanael West

In these present days, now more than any other time in history, we function by the clock and the calendar. "We live according to times, dates, and measurements," the writing duo of Marie D. Jones and Larry Flaxman say, in their *11:11 The Time Prompt Phenomenon*. "We are constantly being bombarded with numbers and patterns," via landline and cell phones, computer passwords, appliances, bank accounts, checkbooks, credit cards, ATM pin numbers, alarm codes, Social Security numbers, clocks, watches, TV channels, radio frequencies, agriculture, architecture, manufacturing, mining, marketing, advertising, music, art, all sciences, the medical field, the judicial system, prison ID bracelets, education, travel, passports, vehicles, entertainment, and the IRS; in short, any and everything involved with socio-politico-economic characteristics; not to mention our personal driver's licenses, license plates, phone numbers, house numbers, birthdays, anniversaries, our ages and goals, and " . . . even our ranking within a family, such as a third child," adds the MacGregors. Numbers have become fundamental to our civilization as a whole.

"Numbers are considered to be the language of the universe," Linn explains. "All that exists in the physical cosmos, every atom, molecule, dimension, or form, can be represented by numbers." Surely you've heard the expression that there's a mathematical explanation for everything; that numbers can explain the structure of the universe. Dr. Ira Progoff shows that the physical world is given order and pattern via mathematics. "Numbers have the power to shape, form, describe, manifest, and transform," say Jones and Flaxman. " Numbers truly are the key to the universe.""

Throughout time, numbers have also been associated with mystic significance, spiritual qualities, and daily events. And synchronicity loves numbers. "You know that there is no such thing as an unlucky number, although many people believe that 13 is unlucky. (It is my brother's favorite number.) Nor is there an unlucky event, such as breaking a mirror, or stepping on a crack, or opening an umbrella indoors, or a black cat crossing your path. (I had a pet black cat named Licorice.) Superstitions are carried down through the ages via family lore, old wives' tales, and urban legends (good luck horseshoes, four-leaf clovers, wishing on a star, fingers crossed, knock on wood, and so forth).

It is said that numbers hold within them certain vibrational energies and symbolic meanings, which can serve as guideposts. When you experience particular numbers—or number sequences—that come into your life, you know there are way too many for them to be a coincidence. The universe is communicating with you, to help awaken your consciousness. Repeating numbers are reassuring.

As James points out, when certain numbers keep showing up, you invariably feel " . . . that something important, perhaps even divine, is trying to communicate through the numerical symbol." Number clusters are considered to be wake-up calls, urging you to *pay attention*. If, for instance, you're hearing or seeing 911 everywhere, perhaps you're being warned about an upcoming emergency or personal crisis.

Pay attention to repetitive numbers. If a number keeps appearing to you, in various forms, check out the corresponding meaning. (One night I kept dreaming of the numbers 22211. I was so afraid I'd forget the numbers by morning, that I got up, wrote it on my calendar, and checked their meaning. Needless to say, I was extremely pleased with the message!) When persistent numbers occur, Soliel says that her antennae immediately goes up. The MacGregors agree, saying, "If you Google 11:11, about 200 million sites come up. Obviously, there is considerable interest in these numbers, and this cluster is among the most common." Adding: "Confirmations and warnings seem to accompany this cluster."

Ascending numbers denote improvement (12:34). Note that the meaning you give to any number or number cluster, can be determined by your family, culture, religion, or your age, as well as your own experiences. Some people have their own lucky number! Like the California Power 5 Scratchers commercial says, "When you find a number that works for you—stick with it!"

Number clusters of threes—3, 33, 333—are prominent.

3:33

Angel (my daughter-in-law) and her two grown daughters, have matching **3:33** tattoos on their inner wrists. Not because of the more popular trinities of mind/body/spirit, or mother/father/child, or the Holy Trinity of Father/Son/Holy Ghost, but in the memory of Angel's mother.

Angel's mother died when she was eleven years old. Later, her father died when Angel was nineteen, and she was devastated. Overcome with sadness, she moved out of her stepmother's house, and settled in South Beach, Florida. But she was having a difficult time adjusting to life without both parents.

During the first 11 months of her adventure, she had a recurring dream—three or four times a week, always the same dream. She would be dreaming that she was asleep in her apartment (which she was), and the phone would ring, and she would awaken and answer it (during the dream). The phone was on her nightstand, alongside her alarm clock. The time was always 3:33. In her dream, she would always answer the call. It was always her mother, who had died many years prior. And her message was always the same. Her mother would say, "I know you are having a hard time, and feeling alone, but we have not left you. We are always with you."

The last time Angel had the dream, she actually woke up, and when she looked at the clock, it was 3:33. She immediately answered the phone, as she had so many times in her dream, but it was only a dial tone. She laughed to herself, thinking, "Did I really think she would be on the other end?" As soon as she had that thought, she felt a chill in the air, and an overpowering scent, that she knew had to be her mother: White Shoulders perfume!!! Her favorite! Angel sat quietly for about 45 seconds, and tried to process what was happening. She then said out loud, "Mom, I know you are here, but it's kind of freaking me out!" As soon as the words left her mouth, the chill and the scent dissipated, and she never had that dream again.

To this day, whenever Angel or her daughters see the numbers 33 or 333, they think of her mother, Gayle. And they know she is with them. Oddly, I see 33 and 333 quite often, myself.

Numbers are peculiar animals.
They can unlock secrets,
split atoms,
reveal the inner workings of people and machines,
or draw patterns
of astounding complexity and beauty.
—Dame Anita Roddick

Pythagoras, the ancient Greek philosopher and mathematician (known as the "father of numbers"), said, "All is number." He believed that each number held a mystical significance. Each number is a symbol, showing capacity and spiritual essence. By checking out the numbers that spontaneously show up in your life, you can find direction, understanding, and help. The following short compilation list of number meanings is offered via Linn, the MacGreggors, Millman, Upczak, and Venefic

NUMBERS SYMBOLOGY

0 = wholeness, contemplation, unity, spiritual gifts

1= individualism, independence, new beginnings, creativity, self- development, valuing oneself, oneness, dynamic, pioneering, unique, self, success, takes charge, leadership, initiate, or too strong, domineering, ego

2 = the power of choice, crossroads, decisions, judgment, the balance of opposites, dynamic attraction, companion, partnerships, cooperation, harmony, teamwork, planning, tact, aware, unite, or meddling

3 = expression, expansion, communication, growth, cooperation, optimism ("third time's the charm"), new adventures, self-expression, curiosity, creative, imagination, intuition, travel, social, lucky events, positive thinking, generosity, multi-talented, reward, success

4 = security, order, foundation, stability, solidity, grounded, hard work, self-discipline, provider,

wholeness, organization, practical, productivity, calmness, home, roots, protector, persistence, patience

5 = adventure, breaking free from boundaries, exploration, new direction, travel, motion, excitement, change, constant movement, activity, freedom, friends, glamour, passion, excitement, action, creativity, self expression, communication, versatility, responsible indulgence, wake- up call, wisdom, or impulsive, unpredictability, scattered, primitive, erratic

6 = service, social responsibility, harmony, balance, love, self, family, children, home, environment, practical, conventional, safety, duty, sincerity, beauty, the arts, generosity, health, truth, calm, compassion, or strong need to be needed

7 = seeker, thinker, endings leading to good beginnings, solitude, inner life, contemplation, introspection, awareness, truth, wisdom, imagination, exploring the spiritual, mystery, perfection, security, safety, rest, and magical forces (the heptagram, a 7-pointed star—a sheriff's star—is the traditional star for warding off evil). The number seven plays significant role in mythology, as well as religion (Christianity, Islam. Hinduism, and others. See pages 118-121 In Jones and Flaxman's *11:11 The Time Prompt Phenomenon*.) Seven is an

auspicious number: 7 colors in the rainbow, 7 chords in the diatonic scale, 7 days in the week, 7 continents in our world, 7 wonders of the ancient world, 7 seas, 7 chakras, 7 stars in the Big Dipper, 7 dwarfs in the *Snow White* fairy tale, and so on. Pythagoras called 7 the perfect number, because of 3 and 4, the triangle and the square.

8 = business, financial success, reaching goals, ambition, determined, personal power, wealth, abundance, infinity, reward, disciplined, authority, leadership, business, success, determination, material prosperity, renew, responsibility, cosmic consciousness or greed, winning at all costs

9 = attainment, satisfaction, accomplishment, completion, endings, transition, compassion, tolerance, selflessness, power, inventiveness, influence, wisdom, humanitarian, resourceful, devoted, healing, higher vision and purpose, dedication, transformation, immortality

10 = perfection, accomplishment, solution, new beginning

11 = a wake-up call, new beginning, purity, intuition, vision, balance, sensitive, highly creative, artistic and inventive, a leader, great success, higher ideals, clairvoyance, spiritual

healing, illumination, a Master/Power number denoting a spiritual path

12 = Twelve is an auspicious number, as Millman points out: "12 hours on a clock, 12 inches to a foot, 12 months in a year, 12 days of Christmas, 12 signs of the zodiac, 12- Step programs, 12 labors of Hercules, 12 jurors to dispense justice, the 12 tribes of Israel, 12 gates to the city of Jerusalem, and 12 disciples of Jesus."

13 = The number 13 is a mixed bag of good or bad generating power. Dark symbolism occurs in the Norse, ancient Greek, Egyptian, Persian, Zorostrianism, and early Christian myths. Whereas lucky 13s are expressed in Italy, Roman Catholicism, Sikhism, Judaism, Shia, Mesoamerican and Chinese classics. Even today, the number 13 implies uncertainty, hesitation, fickleness, or transformation—the end of something (death), and a renewal, an important change. Many hotels do not acknowledge a 13th floor, skipping from the twelfth floor directly to the fourteenth floor. Nor do they have thirteen steps. Most guests do not even notice. But you do notice Friday the 13th when it rolls around. According to Toni Corsi's *Superstitions* website, 80 percent of high-rises also lack a 13th floor. In addition, airports skip gate 13, airplanes have no 13th aisle, hospitals and hotels have no Room 13, and many cities don't have a 13th street or

avenue. And consider the ill-fated Apollo 13. Who knew that superstitions still had such a great hold on people? He also states that if you have 13 letters in your name, that you have the devil's luck (citing Jack the Ripper, Charles Manson, Theodore Bundy, Jeffrey Dahmer, and Albert DeSalvo). Yikes! But I have nothing to fear from the number 13, as I was just informed that my book, *Seizing the Teachable Moment* (2015), was listed and critiqued in the *BookMad* Digital Magazine, May, 2016 issue, on page 13!

22 = unlimited potential in any area, blends vision and creativity, disciplined, gifted manifestor, master builder

33 = master teacher, all things are possible, great communicator, helps others to reach their goals, transcendence, enlightenment

44 = growth through challenge, reassess attitude and thought patterns, be more proactive

55 = cultivating self-trust, building a stronger foundation, master through higher wisdom and intuition or instability and flux

66 = contemplation, meditation, searching for a larger purpose or more meaning in daily life, transmutation and expanding consciousness, kundalini awakenings

77 = personal growth, more open, endings leading to good beginnings, solitude, deep connection with inner world, mystic traveler, seeker, spiritual happenings, rapid awakening, expanding consciousness

88 = self-disciplined, inspired, encouraging, assertive, groundbreaker, trail blazer, pioneer, keeps looking up, teaches principles, high spiritual energy and awareness

99 = idealism, seeing bigger picture, positive visionar

000 = harmony; grand life plan or mission

111 = a wake-up call, cosmic confirmation that you're headed in the right direction, new beginnings; suggesting that the change you are contemplating is the right thing to do, The Celestine Vision website message board defines 111 or 1111 as "Energy flow of water, money, sex, kundalini, magnetic.

222 = forging ahead in the right direction, a Manifestation number, you are in the moment, positive impact, personal luck, empowerment, charisma, relations, partnership, speak up; trust your inner voice, you light up a room

333 = truth, the union of mind, body, and spirit, balanced, in the zone, feeling fulfilled by life, blessed, Yes!

444 = prosperity, abundance, nothing to fear, all is well, the power of God's love; supported by angels, angels are talking to you, nudging you to the next level, or in a different direction

555 = life-altering, positive change; moving forward

666 = the mark of the beast (the devil or the antichrist), which is in the Bible's Book of Revelation in the New Testament, chapter 13. It is considered to be an extremely negative number, or regain your balance

777 = a very high spiritual number, learning or teaching a more spiritually conscious way of being, Congratulations!

888 = end in harmony, Shamanic energy, deeper esoteric knowledge, bridging the blocks to inter-dimensional communication, deepening understanding of the mystery of the universe

999 = a master number, completion, ending jobs or relationships that no longer serve you, a profound lesson occurring for accelerated growth, new doors opening

1010 = the Alpha and Omega number, beginnings and endings, full of promise

1111 = a manifestation number, the correct path for your spiritual journey; heightened awareness, your reason to be here, the gateway, you are a Lightworker here to uplift consciousness and restore harmony, you are on the right path, you are a bridge, you are in the moment

1212 = the Higher Realms, new ways of being and experiencing, service for humanity and all living things (As mentioned earlier, the TV version of my book, *The Bogeyman: Stalking And Its Aftermath*, aired on the Investigation Discovery channel on 12/12/12.)

> *Every culture has contributed to math,*
> *just as it has contributed to language;*
> *numbers belong to everyone.*
> —Daniel Tammet

AFTERWORD

Life is symbolic,
so keep interpreting.
—Avia Venefica

Know that the sense of connectedness that coincidences, synchronicities, dreams, signs and symbols can bring, can enlarge your understanding of the world. They expand your perception, allowing you to consider another reality that lies behind the surface of things.

Hopefully, the ending of this book will be a new beginning for you. One in which you recognize that you have had such subtle nudges and experiences in your life; that you look forward to experiencing and enjoying coincidences and synchronicities on a regular basis; that you trust and use your intuition; that you work at translating your dream messages; that you consider your color choices; that you keep an eye pealed for various signs and symbols along the way; and that you have the courage to live a more open-minded life, as you step back and observe the bigger picture. Understand that life proceeds out of your intentions for it, so if you're not receiving a sign, set a firm intention and call it forth via an affirmation: "*I am* going to receive a sign!" Look for possibilities.

It is my intent that this book is a kind of heart-to-heart communication with you, having to do with clearing the way for a more fulfilling and rewarding life. Know that there is no such thing as separation in the world. Find the courage to simply pose questions to yourself and to the Universe, and confidently watch and listen for answers. Keep your eyes wide open, and your ear to the ground. Live with purpose and intention.

My sincere wish is that you keep your wonder and awe alive, as you continue your journey for a rich flow of happiness and joy. Make the choice for your wholehearted participation in conscious living. Work to expand in love and creativity every day, as you open to a deep sense of connection with all. Embrace the oneness of the Universe.

And, in the end,
It's not the years in your life that count.
It's the life in your years.
—Abraham Lincoln

REFERENCES

Alden, Andrew. (2016). *Geologic sayings and proverbs*. Retrieved on May 18, 2016 from geology.about.com

All Totems. (2012-2015). *Animal totems A—Z*. Retrieved May 3, 2016 from http://alltotems.com/

Andrews, Ted, *Animal-Wise: Understanding the Language of Animal Messengers and Companions*. (Jackson, TN: Dragonhawk Publishing, 2009). pp. 25,168-234,

_____. *Nature-Speak: Signs, Omens and Messages in Nature*. (Jackson, TN: Dragonhawk Publishing, 2004). pp. 11, 189-221, 300-312, 332-370, 412.

Arruda, Nancy. (2004-2014). *List of animals and their key words*. Retrieved April 28, 2016 from nancy@universalsky.com

_____. (2004-2014). *List of birds and their key words*. RetrievedApril 28, 2016 from nancy@universalsky.com

_____. (2004-2014). *List of insects and their key words*. Retrieved April 27, 2016 from <u>nancy@universalsky.com</u>

_____. (2004-2014). *List of reptiles and their key words*. Retrieved April 28, 2016 from <u>nancy@universalsky.com</u>

Baldacci, David, *The Last Mile*. (New York: Grand Central Publishing, 2016). p. 221.

Barnard, George Mathieu, *The Search for 11:11: A Journey into the spirit World*. (Australia: 11.11 Publishers, 2004). pp. 15, 88, 122.

Beadage. (1998-2016). *Gemstone meanings and properties*. Retrieved April 6, 2016 from http://beadage.net/gemstones/

Bell, Craig S., *Comprehending Coincidence: Synchronicity and Personal Transformation*. (West Chester, PA: Chrysalis Books, 2000). pp.136-137.

Beitman, Bernard D., M.D. *Connecting with Coincidence: The New Science for Using Synchronicity and Serendipity in Your Life.*

(Deerfield Beach, FL: Health Communications, Inc.). pp. III, 126, 210-211, 243, 257.

Bohm. David, *Wholeness and the Implicate Order.* (Abingdon, U.K.: Taylor and Francis Publishers, reissue 2002).

Bolen, Jean Shinoda, M.D., *The Tao of Psychology: Synchronicity and the Self.* (New York: HarperOne, 2004). p.49.

Bro, Harmon Hartzell, Dr. *Edgar Cayce on Dreams.* (New York: Castle Books, 1968). pp. 24, 59, 105, 111, 114, 122, 135, 137, 144, 148, 160.

Burchard, Brendon, *The Charge: Activating the 10 Human Drives That Make You Feel Alive.* (New York: Free Press, 2012). pp. 21, 87.

Burnham, Sophy. *The Art of Intuition: Cultivating Your Inner Wisdom.* (New York: TarcherPerigee, 2011). pp. 3, 46 118, 145.

Campbell, Rebecca, *Light is the New Black: A Guide to Answering Your Soul's Calling and Working Your Light.* (Carlsbad, CA: Hay House, 2015.) p. 86.

Cao, Jerry. (June 11, 2015). *12 colours and the emotions they evoke.* Retrieved May 12, 2016 from www.creativebloq.com/

web-design/12- colours-and-emotions-they-evoke-61515112

Cherry, Kendra. (updated April 26, 2016). *Color psychology: how colors impact moods, feelings, and behaviors.* Retrieved on May 20, 2016 from https://verywell.com

Chopra, Deepak, M.D. *The Spontaneous Fulfillment of Desire: Harnessing the Infinite Power of Coincidence.* (New York: Harmony Books, 2003). pp. 28, 34, 39, 60,120, 140, 136, 137.

"Coloring Your World," *Cancer Fighters Thrive.* Summer, 2016: 50-51. Print.

Colton, Ann Ree, *Watch Your Dreams: A Master Key and Reference Book for All Initiates of the Soul, the Mind, and the Heart.* (Glendale, CA: ARC Publishing, 1973). pp.13, 95, 131-169.

Cordz, Emily. (no date). *8 popular gemstones and their meanings.* Retrieved April 6, 2016 from http:// www.outofstress.com/list-gemstones-meanings/

Corsi, Tony. (1998-2000). *Unusual Trivia Collection: Superstitions.* Retrieved May 3, 2016 from www.corsinet.com

Day, Laura. *Practical Intuition: How to Harness the Power of your Instinct and Make it Work for You.* (New York: Villard, 1996). pp. 50, 60, 84, 86, 90, 174.

Ecoist (2016). *7 Color-changing wonders of the animal kingdom.* Retrieved May 10, 2016 from Momtastic WebEcoist at webecoist. momtastic.   com/2009/02/22/2009/02/08/ amazing-natural-formations-phenomena/

Eisenbraun, Chris. (July 4, 2000). *The symbols: one word at a time.* Retrieved May 3, 2016 from The online symbolism dictionary

Elert, Glenn, Editor. (2006). *Number of colors distinguishable by the human eye.* Retrieved April 10, 2016 from: hhtp://hypertextbook.com/ facts/2006/jennifertLeong.shtml

Farrell, Joseph Pierce, *Manifesting Michelangelo: The Story of a Modern- Day Miracle—that May Make All Change Possible.* (New York: Atria Books, 2011). pp. 63-64.

50states (2016). *50states.com state flowers list.* Retrieved April 11, 2016 from http:// www.50states.com/flower.htm

Fraser, Amy E. (May 9, 2007). *Exalted Beauty: Pearl Symbolism.* Retrieved May 5, 2016 from hhttps:// plus.google.com/+Blogger/

Freud, Sigmund, *The Interpretation of Dreams*. (New York: AVM, 1965).

Gaulden, Albert Clayton, *Signs and Wonders: Finding Peace, Joy, and Direction from Coincidences, Synchronicities, and Angel Murmurs— and Other Ways God Speaks*. (New York: Atria, 2003). pp. 12, 69, 79.

Gems, Emily, (no date). *The meaning of color*. Retrieved April 6, 2016 from https: //crystal-cure.com/color.html

GemSelect. (2005-2016). *Gemstone meanings*. Retrieved April 6, 2016 from http://www.genselect.com/other-info/gemstone-meanings.php

Gemstone Dictionary. (2007-2013). *Gemstone meanings and properties*. Retrieved April 6, 2016 from http://gemstone-dictionary.com/genstones-meanings.php

Gift Tree (2016). *Flower meanings, colors, and symbolic meaning*. Retrieved March 23, 2016 from https://www.gifttree.com/gifts/flowers/flower-meanings.php

Gladwell, Malcolm, *Blink: The Power of Thinking Without Thinking*. (New York: Little, Brown, 2005). pp. 14, 17, 50, 71,107, 108, 122, 194-195.

Greater Good (2000-2016). *Warning colors in the animal world*. Retrieved May 10, 2016 from TheRainforestSite.com

Halberstam, Yita & Judith Leventhal, *Small Miracles: Extraordinary Coincidences from Everyday Life.* (Holbrook, MS: Adams Media Corporation, 1997), pp. vii, 58, 103.

_____.*Small Miracles II: Heartwarming Gifts of Extraordinary Coincidences.* (Holbrook, MS: Adams Media Corporation, 1998). pp. vii, 58, 103, 115.

Harris, Elena, Editor. (2012-2015). *Spirit animals and animal totems*. Retrieved May 3, 2016 from www.spiritanimal.info/

Hartmann, Thom, *The Prophet's Way: A Guide to Living in the Now.* (Rochester, VT: Park Street Press, 2004). p. 71.

Heckler, Richard A., Ph.D., *Crossings: Everyday People, Unexpected Events, and Life-Affirming Change.* (New York: Harcourt Brace & Company, 1998). pp. 111, 112, 130, 153.

Hendricks, Guy, *Conscious Living: Finding Joy in the Real World.* (San Francisco: HarperSanFrancisco, 2000). pp. 66, 74, 81.

Hilburn, Scott. (2016). "The Argyle Sweater: Chameleon Gossip." *Long Beach Press Telegram*, 5, April, 2016. Print.

Hopcke, Robert H., MFT, *There Are No Accidents: Synchronicity and the Stories of Our Lives.* (New York: Riverhead Books, 1997.) pp. 6, 7, 11, 13, 21, 23, 49, 104, 107, 126, 171.

Ingerman, Sandra & Llyn Roberts. *Speaking with Nature: Awakening to the Deep Wisdom of the Earth.* (Rochester, VT: Bear & Company, 2015). p. 263.

Intenders of the Highest Good. (May 28, 2016). *A vision for animals.* Retrieved on May 28, 2016 from The Vision Alignment Project at visionalignmentproject.com

Jones, Marie D. & Larry Flaxman. *11:11 The Time Prompt Phenomenon: The Meaning Behind Mysterious Signs, Sequences, and Synchronicities.* (Pompton Plains, NJ: New Page Books, 2009). pp. 16, 17, 26, 62, 118-121, 211.

Joseph, Frank, *Synchronicity and You: Understanding the role of Meaningful Coincidence in Your Life.* (Boston: Element, 1999). pp. 3, 26-27, 57, 75, 94, 153, 187.

Koch-Sheras, Phyllis R., Amy Lemley, & Peter L. Sheras, Ph.D., *The Dream Sourcebook & Journal: A Guide to the Theory and Interpretation of Dreams.* (New York: Barnes & Noble, 2000). pp. xiii, xx.

Lehner, Ernst & Johanna, *Folklore and Symbolism of Flowers, Plants and Trees.* (New York: Tudor Publishing, 1960). pp.15,

Lembo, Margaret Ann, *The Essential Guide to Crystals, Minerals, and Stones.* (Woodbury, MN: Llewellyn Worldwide). p. 9.

Linn, Denise, *The Secret Language of Signs: How to Interpret the Coincidences and Symbols in Your Life.* (New York: Ballantine, 1996). pp. 3, 6, 26, 27, 42, 48, 59, 61, 66, 69, 82-288.

Love, Presley (2016). *Universe of symbolism*: signs, symbols, and totems. Retrieved April 26, 2016 from www.universeofsymbolism.com

MacGregor, Trish & Rob, *The Synchronicity Highway: Exploring Coincidence, the Paranormal, and Alien Contact.* (Hertford, NC: Crossroad Press, 2013). pp. 45, 47, 49, 257.

_____. *Synchronicity and the Other Side: Your Guide to Meaningful Connections with the Afterlife.* (Avon, MS: Adams Media, 2011). pp. 17, 61, 72, 79, 142-144, 147.

_____. *The Seven Secrets of Synchronicity: Your Guide to Finding Meaning in Signs Big and Small*. (Avon, MS: Adams Media, 2010). pp. xv, 27, 29, 89, 91-97, 178, 191.

_____. (October 9, 2010). *Synchronicity* blog. Retrieved on May 19, 2016 from http://blog.synchrosecrets.com/?p=754

Marcoux, Alex, *Lifesigns: Tapping the Power of Synchronicity, Serendipity and Miracles*. (Littleton, CO: Jenness, 2012). pp. xix, 3, 27, 33, 35. 36.

Mascarenhas, Cheryl (updated February 13, 2016). *Bird symbolism and their meanings*. Retrieved April 29, 2016 from Buzzle.com

Matlins, Antoinette, P.G. *Colored Gemstones: The Antoinette Matlins Buying Guide* (3rd Edition). (Woodstock VT: Gemstone Press, 2010). p. 6.

Meinberg, Sherry L. *A Cluster of Cancers: A Simple Coping Guide for Patients*. (Bloomington, IN: AuthorHouse, 2015).

_____. *Seizing the Teachable Moment*. (Bloomington, IN: AuthorHouse, 2015).

_____. *The Cockroach Invasion*. (Bloomington, IN: Archway Publishing, 2014).

_____. *Breadcrumbs for Beginners: Following the Writing Trail*. (Bloomington, In: Balboa Press, 2014).

_____. *Imperfect Weddings are Best*. (North Charleston, SC: CreateSpace, 2012).

_____. *Recess is Over! No Nonsense Strategies and Tips for Student Teachers and New Teachers* (Charleston, SC: Booksurge, 2010).

_____. *Autism ABC*. (Charleston, SC: Booksurge, 2009).

_____. *Toxic Attention: Keeping Safe from Stalkers, Abusers, and Intruders*. (New York: iUniverse, 2003).

_____. *The Bogeyman: Stalking and its Aftermath*. (New York: iUniverse, 2003). pp. 5-12, 52-55.

Millman, Dan, *Everyday Enlightenment: The Twelve Gateways to Personal Growth*. (New York: Warner Books, 1998). pp. 4, 24-25, 146, 147, 167, 171,189.

Millman, Dan & Doug Childers, *Bridge Between Worlds: Extraordinary Experiences That Changed Lives*. (Navato, CA: New World Library, 2009). p. ix-x.

Moss, Robert, *The Three "Only" Things: Tapping the Power of Dreams, Conincidence, and Imagination.* (Norvato, CA: New World Library, 2007. pp. 20, 26, 45, 64, 115, 130.

National Park—Adventures.com (no date). *United States national parks list.* Retrieved May 1, 2016 from nationalpark-adventures.com/united-states-national-parks.html

National Park Service (2016). *United States national park list.* Retrieved May 1, 2016 from www.nps.gov

Nedha (January 5, 2011, updated May 27, 2015). *Difference between rocks and stones.* Retrieved April 29, 2016 from DifferenceBetween.com

Pearl, Eric, Dr. & Frederick Ponzlov, *Solomon Speaks on Reconnecting Your Life. (Carlsbad, CA: Hay House, 2013).* pp. 6, 24, 38, 51, 57, 69, 75, 80, 108-109,177, 183.

Pearson, Carol Lynn, *Embracing Coincidence: Transforming Your Life Through Synchronicity.* (Salt Lake City, UT: Gibbs Smith Publisher, 2008). p. 15.

Peirce, Penney, *The Intuitive Way: The Definitive Guide to Increasing Your Awareness.* (New York: Atria, 2009).

Progoff, Ira, Dr., *Jung, Synchronicity, and Human Destiny: Noncausal Dimensions of Human Experience* (New York: Delta, 1973).

PsychologyCampus.com (2004-2008). *Carl Jung.* Retrieved April 8, 2016 from: http://www.psychologycanpus.com/dream-psychology/carl-jung.html

Redfield, James, *The Celestine Prophecy.* (New York: Warner Books, 1997). pp. 6-7, 36, 68, 119, 164, 166, 178, 205, 208, 228.

Richo, David, Ph.D., M.F.T, *The Power of Coincidence: How Life Shows Us What We Need to Know.* (Boston: Shambhala Publications, 1998). pp.11, 15, 53, 68.

_____. *Unexpected Miracles: The Gift of Synchronicity and How to Open It.* (New York: Crossroads, 1998). pp. 19, 20, 22, 51, 57, 74, 76, 138.

Rushnell, SQuire, *When God Winks: How the Power of Coincidence Guides Your Life.* (New York: Atria Books, 2001). pp. 2, 4, 13, 22, 23, 159.

_____, *When God Winks at You: How God Speaks Directly to You Through the Power of Coincidence.* (Nashville: Nelson Books, 2006). pp. 3, 4.

Sander, Christin. (2016). *Totem Wisdom: Totem Animal List*. Retrieved April 28, 2016 from TotemWisdom.com

Serpentspeaks (posted September 20, 2012). *How many insects are there in the world?* Retrieved May 8, 2016 fro http://serpentspeaks.wordpress.com/2012/09/20/howmanyinsects

Schulz, Mona Lisa, M.D., Ph.D. *Awakening Intuition: Using Your Mind-Body Network for Insight and Healing.* (New York: Three Rivers Press, 1998). pp. 2, 19, 30, 41-43, 49, 84.

Smashing Tops. (2016). *Animal mimicry.* Retrieved May 10, 2016 from SmashingTops.com

Smithsonian Ocean Portal Team. (2015). *Census of marine life.* Retrieved May 10, 2016 from ocean.si.edu/census-marine-life

Soliel, Mary, *I Can See Clearly Now: How Synchronicity Illuminates Our Lives.* (New York: iUniverse, 2008). pp. 69, 172, 184.

Spangler, David. *Everyday Miracles: The Inner Art of Manifestation.* (New York: Bantam Books, 1996). pp. 43, 46, 52, 68, 69, 70.

State Symbols USA (no date). *The rose: national (U.S.) flower symbol.* Retrieved April 11, 2016 from http://www.statesymbolsusa.org/symbol-or-officially-designated-item/ state-flower/rose

Surprise, Kirby, Dr., *Synchronicity: The Art of Coincidence, Choice, and Unlocking Your Mind.* (Pompton Plains, NJ: New Page Books, 2012). pp. 9, 38.

The Old Farmer's Almanac (1793-2016). *Monthly Flowers.* Retrieved May 1, 2016 from https://www.almanac.com/content/nthlybirthflowers

_____. (1793-2016). *Monthly Birthstones.* Retrieved May 1, 2016 from https://www.almanac.com/content/monthlybirthstones

Thurston, Mark, Dr., *Synchronicity as Spiritual Guidance: All of Life is Working Together to Leave You Little Hints.* (Virginia Beach, VA: ARE Press, 2004). pp. 3-4, 18, 20, 21.

United States National Arboretum. (updated 2010, July 14). *State treesand state flowers.* Retrieved April 11, 2016 from http://www.usna.usda-gov/Gardens/collections/statetreeflower.html

Upczak, Patricia Rose, *Synchronicity, Signs and Symbols.* (Nederland, CO: Synchronicity Publishing, 2001). pp. 20, 50, 71-72, 84-106.

Van Buren, Abigail. "Dear Abby." *Press-Telegram* {Long Beach, CA} 9 June 2016, sec. A:17. Print.

Venefica, Avia (2005-2017). *Animal symbolism.* Retrieved April 19, 2016 from www.whats-your-sign.com

_____. (2005-2017). *Dream symbolism.* Retrieved April 19, 2016 from www.whats-your-sign.com

_____. (2005-2017). *Flower symbolism.* Retrieved March 23, 2016 from www.whats-your-sign.com

_____. (2005-2017). *Spiritual meaning of numbers.* Retrieved May 6, 2016from www.whats-your-sign.com

_____. (2005-2017). *Tree symbolism.* Retrieved April 11, 2016 from www.whats-your-sign.com

_____. (2005-2017). *Symbolic meanings from Nature.* Retrieved May 2, 2016 from www.whats-your-sign.com

Villoldo, Alberto, Ph.D. *One Spirit Medicine: Ancient Ways to Ultimate Wellness.* (Carlsbad, CA: Hay House, 2015). p. 185.

Viorst, Judith, *The Tenth Good Thing About Barney.* (New York: Atheneum, September 30, 1987, with many reprints thereafter).

Vivekananda, Bengali, Swami. *The Complete Works of Swami Vivekananda*. (Calcutta, India: Advaita Ashrama, 1989). p. 72.

Watkins, Susan M., *What a Coincidence! The Wow! Factor in Synchronicity and What it Means in Everyday Life*. (Needham, MS: Moment Point Press,). pp. 19, 47.

Walsch, Neale Donald, *Moments of Grace: When God Touches Our Lives Unexpectedly*. (Charlottesville, VA: Hampton Roads, 2001). pp.13, 22, 37, 55, 70, 74, 91,187.

_____. (2000). *Awakening Intuition*. Retrieved April 5, 2016 from awakening-intuition.com

_____. (no date). *I believe God wants you to know*. Retrieved May 4, 2016 from today@ nealedonaldwalsch.com

Wanless, James. *Little Stone: Your Friend for Life*. (Boston, MS: Element, 1999).

Weaver, Rheyanne. (March 30, 2012). *The link between clothing choices and emotional states*. Retrieved May 12, 2016 from GoodTherapy.org

White, E.B., *Charlotte's Web*. (New York: Harper Brothers, October 25, 1952, with numerous reprints thereafter).

Wikipedia (no date). *List of U.S. state flags, seals, coats of arms*. Reviewed May 2, 2016 from Wikipedia.

_____. (modified April, 2016). *List of U.S. state minerals, rocks, stones, and gemstones*. Reviewed on May 1, 2016 from Wikipedia.

_____. (modified 28, April, 2016). *Animal camouflage*. Retrieved on May 10, 2016 from Wikipedia.

Wilcock, David, *The Synchronicity Key: The Hidden Intelligence Guiding the Universe and You*. (New York: Dutton, 2013). p. viii.

Williams, David B. (November 2, 2011—2016). *Rock and stone: Is there a difference?* retrieved on April 29, 2016 from GeologyWriter,com

WiseGeek Team. (2003-2016). *How many species of animals are there?* Retrieved May 11, 2016 from wisegeek.org

Zyistra, Matthew J. 2014. Exploring meaningful nature experience, connectedness with nature and the revitalization of transformative education for sustainability. PhD dissertation, Dept. Conservation Ecology. Stellenbosch University, Stellenbosch.

INDEX

O

O'Keeffe, Georgia 17, 103

P

Pearl, Eric, Ph.D. 11
Ponzlov, Frederick 11, 302
Progoff, Ira, Ph.D. 275
Pythagoras 279, 282

R

Redfield, James 18, 92,
    94, 303
repetition 7, 12, 15, 17, 108
Richo, David, Ph.D. 303
Robinson, Sugar Ray 79
rocks vii, 61, 137, 180, 181,
    187, 189, 302, 308
Rushnell, SQuire 7, 303

S

Schultz, Mona Lisa, M.D.,
    Ph.D. 65
Sheras, Peter L., Ph.D.
    79, 299
signs iii, v, vii, 7, 24, 37, 72,
    73, 79, 97, 102, 105,
    107, 108, 109, 110,

111, 112, 113, 114,
    115, 116, 122, 126,
    140, 166, 169, 182,
    195, 199, 214, 218,
    252, 257, 283, 289,
    290, 291, 296, 298,
    299, 300, 305, 306
Soliel, Mary 23, 304
Spangler, David 5, 114, 304
states 4, 6, 34, 39, 43, 56,
    66, 68, 71, 72, 78, 90,
    97, 115, 116, 117, 118,
    121, 122, 126, 140,
    163, 174, 175, 187,
    189, 196, 197, 199,
    225, 249, 260, 261,
    262, 284, 295, 302,
    304, 305, 307, 308
stones vii, 59, 80, 137, 180,
    181, 182, 183, 185,
    187, 188, 189, 191,
    299, 302, 307, 308
Surprise, Kirby, Ph.D. 9, 25
Suzuki, D.T. 6
symbols iii, v, vii, 66, 77, 78,
    89, 108, 115, 116, 140,
    153, 154, 158, 170,
    174, 193, 195, 196,
    197, 200, 201, 202,
    203, 213, 225, 228,
    229, 251, 252, 276,

W

Printed in the United States
By Bookmasters